MODERN FRENCH MUSIC

(*Musée National d' Art Moderne*; Photo. J. Masson)

Picasso's Curtain for the Ballet 'Parade'

MODERN
FRENCH MUSIC

From Fauré to Boulez

ROLLO MYERS

PRAEGER PUBLISHERS
New York · Washington

BOOKS THAT MATTER

Published in the United States of America in 1971
by Praeger Publishers, Inc.,
111 Fourth Avenue, New York, N.Y. 10003

© 1971 in England by Basil Blackwell

This book is published in Great Britain by
Basil Blackwell & Mott under the title *Modern
French Music: Its Evolution and Cultural Background
from 1900 to the Present Day* (ISBN 0 631 13020 9)

Library of Congress Catalog Card Number: 77-154606

Printed in Great Britain

'Je travaille à des choses qui ne seront comprises
que par les petits-enfants du XXe siècle . . .'

Debussy

'Le culte des valeurs spirituelles est à la base
de toute société qui se prétend civilisée, et la
musique, parmi les arts, en est l'expression la
plus sensible et la plus élevée.'

Albert Roussel

'For myself, I cannot begin to take an interest
in the phenomenon of music except in so far as
it emanates from the integral man.'

Stravinsky

CONTENTS

LIST OF PLATES

	1900	1910	1920	1930	1940	1950	1960	1970
1845 FAURÉ			—1924					
1851 d'INDY				—1931				
1862 DEBUSSY		—1918						
1865 DUKAS				—1935				
1866 SATIE			—1925					
1867 KOECHLIN						1950		
1869 ROUSSEL				—1937				
1875 RAVEL				—1937				
1885 VARÈSE							—1965	
1892 MILHAUD								
1892 HONEGGER						—1955		
1899 AURIC								
1899 POULENC							1963	
SAUGUET	b. 1901							
JOLIVET	b. 1905							
MESSIAEN	b. 1908							
BOULEZ			b. 1925					

CHART REPRESENTING LIFE SPANS OF COMPOSERS MENTIONED IN THE TEXT

PROLOGUE

The dawn of the twentieth century found music in Europe in a state of uneasy transition, facing, Janus-like, in two directions at once: forward to a future bright with prospects of new worlds to conquer in the realms of sound, with at the same time a backward glance tinged with *fin-de-siècle* nostalgia and a reluctance to make a final break with the past.

There had been, it is true, two major break-throughs in nineteenth-century music since the death of Beethoven in 1827—one brought about by Hector Berlioz in France at the beginning of the century, and the other by Richard Wagner towards the end; but the influence of the latter was not only far more immediate (Berlioz received little recognition in his life-time) but was to make itself felt for a long time.

Yet in most European countries there remained a hard core of conservatism, or at least a disinclination to stray too far from the beaten path—the path laid down by generations of nineteenth-century composers who between them had shaped what had come to be the more or less generally accepted idiom of the day. How this resistance to new ideas and new techniques was gradually overcome is the story of the evolution of music during the first six decades of the twentieth century. And although in these pages we are specifically concerned with the contribution made to this new musical renaissance by one country—France—it would be pertinent first of all to glance briefly at the general situation in the various European countries at the turn of the century (which we have chosen as our starting-point); this could be summed up roughly as follows.

In Germany, where the last link with the classical past had just been severed by the death of Johannes Brahms in 1897, the chief representatives of what might be called the old school were composers like Max Reger and Hans Pfitzner. Yet already there were signs that a revolution was on the way, for there was now a new voice that spoke for Germany in the person of the young Richard Strauss who at that time represented the avant-garde of European music. Six of his most famous Tone Poems—*Don Juan, Tod und Verklärung, Till Eulenspiegel, Zarathustra, Don Quixote* and *Heldenleben*—were written before he was thirty-five between 1888 and 1898, and proclaimed him as a phenomenally gifted musician and a dynamic force to be reckoned with; and by the year 1900 he was already at work on his second opera (*Feuersnot*). In these works he displayed an exceptional virtuosity in his handling of large orchestral forces, though his unashamed adherence in all of them to a literary, or anecdotal 'programme' (hence the term Tone Poem) caused eyebrows to be raised in certain academic circles where the cult of 'pure' music was still in vogue.

In Austria Gustav Mahler and Anton Bruckner were writing their classical-romantic symphonies and Hugo Wolf was pouring out his inspired Lieder; Arnold Schoenberg had just composed his first big work, the *Gurrelieder*, but his music was still tonal.

In the Iberian peninsula Enrique Granados and Isaac Albeniz were putting Spanish music on the map again after its long slumber, preparing the way for Manuel de Falla who was later to become the most distinguished Spanish composer of his day.

Music in the Netherlands in the nineteenth century was orientated mainly towards France; and this was especially true of Belgian (Walloon) composers like Joseph Jongen and Victor Vreuls, who were active round the turn of the century but who did not claim in any way to be 'advanced'.

In Italy Giuseppe Verdi had just died (1901), and the leading operatic composers of the day were Pietro Mascagni, Ruggiero Leoncavallo and Giacomo Puccini, whose famous opera *La Tosca* was first performed in 1900. The influence of the two men who were later to become the pioneers of modern music in Italy, Gian Francesco Malipiero and Alfredo Casella, had not yet begun to make itself felt as their careers were only just beginning, so it was Puccini who in the eyes of the world represented Italian music.

Turning now to Central Europe, the year 1904 was marked by the death of Antonin Dvořák, who, since the death of Bedřich Smetana, had dominated the scene in Czecho-Slovakia (or Bohemia as it was then called) and established himself as one of Europe's greatest composers; while in Poland Karol Szymanowski was just starting on a career that was to bring him fame and incidentally give Polish music a new lease of life.

In Russia, as the new century dawned, there were three survivors of the original Five (the 'Mighty Handful') who had created the Nationalist movement which had won for Russian music world-wide fame—Nikolai Rimsky-Korsakov, Mily Balakirev and César Cui; but of these only the first two were still actively creative. The year 1900 in fact saw the first performance of one of Rimsky-Korsakov's finest operas, *Tsar Saltan*.

About the same time a new voice in Russian music, unlike anything that had been heard before, was beginning to impose itself—that of Alexander Skriabin, who seemed to have invented a new harmonic language in his first symphonies and sonatas in order to give expression to the mystical ideas and visions by which he was obsessed which gave to his music an almost hysterically emotional quality that was new in European music. It was an isolated, and in many ways remarkable phenomenon, and also a striking example of the desire to enlarge the vocabulary of music that from now on was to be the main concern of so many twentieth-century composers.

Further north, in Finland, Jean Sibelius had already written *The Swan of Tuonela*, *Finlandia* and his Second Symphony (1901); Edvard Grieg in Norway was writing his last songs and piano pieces, while the Dane Carl Nielsen was introducing a new note of modernism into Scandinavian music and had just produced the second of his six symphonies (1902) entitled *The Four Temperaments*.

In England it was a period of transition, with Sir Hubert Parry and Sir Charles Stanford, the last representatives of the old Victorian era, still playing an important part in British music on the one hand, while on the other new talents were emerging in the persons of Edward Elgar, Frederick Delius, Gustav Holst and Ralph Vaughan Williams, who were the pioneers of the remarkable musical renaissance in Britain that began with the twentieth century. To the two latter especially belongs the credit of freeing British music once and for all from the German-inspired sources on which it had largely depended during the nineteenth century, and thus preparing the way for a genuinely British school.

The year 1900 was also marked, among other events, by the first performance of Elgar's oratorio *The Dream of Gerontius*, following the success in the previous year of his *Enigma Variations* (both, incidentally conducted by Hans Richter), and by the death of Arthur Sullivan, whose collaboration with William Gilbert had resulted in a succession of witty operettas which have won for their authors a permanent place in the annals of light music.

In England the long reign of Queen Victoria was drawing to its close; elsewhere in Europe emperors and kings and the Tsar were on their thrones at a time of relative political stability; and in France Emile Loubet had just become the seventh President of the French Republic.

And so it is against this general background that we must now begin to examine the state of music in France at this time when, as we have seen, the new century that was dawning seemed already to bear within it the seeds of fruitful new developments that were to affect the art of music, for better or for worse, in the years to come.

CHAPTER ONE

MUSIC AND NATIONALITY

The idea of nationality in music—that is to say of music being made consciously, or rather self-consciously, to express 'nationalist' or 'national' characteristics by the deliberate cultivation of 'folk' elements or by the dramatisation of colourful or heroic episodes in a country's history—is a comparatively recent one. Indeed, until roughly the end of the eighteenth century music had always been a kind of international *lingua franca* spoken with little more than slight variations in accent or inflexions from one end of Europe to the other. In the sixteenth century, for example, a musician from Tudor England would have felt equally at home in Flanders, France or Italy, and the interpretation or appreciation of the music he encountered in those countries would have presented him with no problems. Towards the end of the seventeenth century, however, when the centre of interest began to shift to Germany after the appearance on the scene of giants like Bach and Handel, European music entered on a new phase. The emphasis was not yet on nationalism as such, but the extraordinary upsurge of musical activities of every kind in Germany and Austria, accompanied by a remarkable extension of the current musical vocabulary, seemed to mark the dawn of a new era—an era unique in the annals of music if only because it witnessed the birth of three of the greatest composers of all time, Haydn, Mozart and Beethoven. When these were followed in due course by Schubert, Schumann, Wagner and Brahms, small wonder that during the period between the birth of Bach and the death of Brahms—roughly two hundred years —the supremacy of German music was something that came to be taken for granted and remained unchallenged—at least in *bien pensant* musical circles—long after it had, in fact, ceased to be a vital force in the contemporary scene. This was the prevailing climate until at least the early years of the twentieth century which made it difficult for the music of other countries, however meritorious, to gain recognition except from a small number of discerning and unprejudiced observers.

Thus, to take a simple example, it was a long time before any one discovered that Gabriel Fauré in France was a composer whose songs and piano works could well stand comparison with those of Schumann—or, indeed, that Debussy was a genius who had no counterpart at all in German music or, for that matter, in the music of any other country. It was this state of affairs that accounts for the growing tendency of the smaller countries in Europe towards the end of the nineteenth century to develop a consciously 'national' type of music as a first step towards complete emancipation from the all-pervading influence of Germany. The first to attempt a breakaway of this kind were Bohemia (as it then was), where the example of Bedřich Smetana (1824–1884) was followed by Antonin Dvořák; Hungary, with Liszt, despite his cosmopolitanism, as one of the first to colour his music with folk-loric elements; and above all Russia, where the famous 'Group of Five' (led by Rimsky-Korsakov and Balakirev) deliberately set out to found a 'Nationalist' school to counteract what they considered to be the harmful influence of Germanic music. In England and Scandinavia there were similar movements on a smaller scale, but in France there was nothing strictly comparable, although it was the new music coming from that country that was to secure for France at the beginning of the twentieth century the same kind of position and prestige that had been enjoyed by Germany during the nineteenth. At the same time, this new French music, as I have said, was in no sense coloured by any self-consciously 'national' aspirations; still less did it draw on 'folk' elements as the Czechs and Russians did in order to make their point. Debussy, for example, had very decided views on this subject. He had been particularly impressed, during a visit he paid to Budapest in 1911, by hearing a violinist called Radics play authentic untutored song—a fact that may help to explain why the French are not, strictly speaking, a 'musical' people, although they have produced some very great musicians. Unlike German, Russian or English people, who like to make music themselves for their own satisfaction and to provide their emotions with an outlet, the Frenchman is content to leave these matters to specialists, not liking to do imperfectly *en amateur* what he feels will be much better done by professionals. Undoubtedly in music this attitude leads to a certain sterility and lack of spontaneity among the people as a whole, but it does account for those other qualities which, as we have seen, are present in the best French music.

The whole question of nationality in music is, however, a complex one, and goes deeper than a mere assessment of superficial characteristics; for nationality in music, or in any other art, can manifest itself in many different ways. Thus we are accustomed, for example, to think of the music of Hungary, or Russia, or Spain as being essentially 'national' because the best-known composers belonging to those nations have assimilated in a varying degree the folk-music elements of their respective countries. And yet it would not be difficult to name composers of individual merit whose nationality is not necessarily apparent in their music, whatever their country of origin: not apparent, that is to say, in the sense that they actually make use of definitely 'national' tunes or rhythms. Nevertheless, we may be conscious of an attitude towards music, or a way of writing music, that we somehow associate unmistakably with a given nationality. This is because certain countries have their own musical styles and traditions which do not necessarily owe anything to the influence of the 'popular' or 'folk' element. Thus it is possible to speak, perfectly intelligibly and correctly, of a piece of music being German, or Italian, or French in character, feeling and style, although it may reflect nothing but the personality of the composer, and present, on the surface at least, no features which could be described as characteristically 'national'.

Tzigane music, with which he compared unfavourably
called Hungarian music of certain contemporary compos
cluding Liszt. The latter, he complained (in a lette
Hungarian impresario who had sent him some musi
spite of his genius makes it sound tame. . . . In my opin
should never touch this music. In fact one ought to d
as far as possible from the bungling of the professio
Your young musicians might with advantage turn to i
spiration—not by copying it, but by trying to trans
freedom, its evocative power, its sadness and its rhyth
advice given by Wagner has been very bad for the m
great many countries. One should only use the folk
one's country as a basis, never as a style of writing. A
especially true of your own popular music. Cher
passionately as you like, but do not dress it up in
robes or make it wear gold spectacles! . . . It's only be
love for music—and not only for French music—is I
that I'm always sorry to see its riches wasted, and it
nificance—I might say its national significance—dist

One of the reasons for this distrust of folk-music a
for the 'serious' composer is that French music I
been predominantly aristocratic in its highest man
and owes less than that of most other countries to
sources of inspiration. It has been a music of courts
of the marketplace, and from Rameau to Ravel its
always been intellectual and imaginative rather tha
emotional. All French art shows the same preoccu
form and technique, the same attention to polish a
balance and clarity above all. Like the good craf
the French artist is proud of his *métier*, and it is pe
to this fact that the ruder and more uncultivated fo
such as communal singing, for example—have nev
in France. The genius of the nation expresses it
form or other of sophistication better than in spo

[1] *Claude Debussy: Lettres inédites à André Caplet* (ed. Edwa
Editions du Rocher 1957.) Note to Letter XXI.

A distinction must therefore be established between thematic and stylistic nationalism in music—between, that is to say, the actual musical material in general and the manner of its presentation—in other words, the style of writing peculiar to each individual composer. On the one hand we find composers who rely on the former element and derive their inspiration mainly from folk-music (e.g. Bartók, Janáček, Falla or Vaughan Williams) and on the other, men like Fauré or Debussy, Prokofiev or Hindemith, who do not use specifically national themes, but whose nationality is none the less apparent in their musical language and mental and psychological make-up.

Nowhere can this more indefinable and subtle aspect of nationalism be better studied than in the music of France, and more particularly in the works of composers like, for example, Fauré or Rousssel whose music is so 'French' that foreigners are supposed to be unable to appreciate its great beauties. And yet the Fauré idiom, for example, presents absolutely no features that are specifically French as regards externals; the 'Frenchness' of his music has its roots in the whole tradition of French culture in its widest sense rather than in any particular manifestation of that culture as expressed in a type of melody or rhythm peculiar to the French people. What is revealed in the music of these composers is, in fact, an instinctive aesthetic and intellectual attitude having its roots in an age-long tradition of civilised living and thinking, and an awareness of the essential values implicit in all great art which Roussel expressed so perfectly when he wrote: 'Le culte des valeurs spirituelles est à la base de toute société qui se prétend civilisée, et la musique, parmi les arts, en est l'expression la plus sensible et la plus élevée.'

It is nationalism in this sense, then, in which music, like literature and the other arts, participates inevitably to a greater or less degree, that counts for so much more than the purely 'folk' influence which is more superficial. For there is, after all, such a thing as national culture, although even that, historically considered, is a comparatively recent conception. We have only to reflect that in the early days of music's development in the Western world, that is to say from about A.D. 1200 to 1500, or even later, art literally knew no frontiers. Countries were not divided from one another by rigid boundaries, either economic or artistic, and educated men spoke the same language from London to Rome. There were centres of culture in Oxford, Paris, Bologna or Córdoba, but it was the same *kind* of culture everywhere, and such distinctions for example as 'Latin', 'Teutonic' or 'Nordic' would have been meaningless to the good Europeans of those days. And just as there was only one kind of learning among scholars, so was there only one kind of music known to musicians. First there were the Troubadours; then there was the great polyphonic school of the Netherlands; then the Madrigalists who prepared the way for the instrumental school which reached its culmination in Bach, Haydn and Mozart and their successors in the nineteenth century.

This admittedly rough-and-ready chronology, showing how these three currents stand out from the main stream of music as it gradually developed in importance as an art, also makes it clear that all through these stages musical Europe spoke very much the same language everywhere, and that what we now call national characteristics played a very small part in the arts at that time. The Troubadours flourished wherever there were courts and polite society, and would have been understood anywhere in France or Italy; the polyphonist school had its headquarters in the Low Countries but had ramifications in England as well as Italy; and the art of the Madrigal, though having its origin in Italy, was brought to an equally high perfection by the great Tudor musicians in England in the sixteenth century. And in style and idiom there was little variation from the norm.

It was not, however, until much later, owing to political and economic causes, that 'nationalistic' ideas began gradually to emerge and make themselves felt in the art and literature of certain countries; and not, as we have seen, until the nineteenth century that nationalism with a capital N, in music as in everything else, began to be deliberately cultivated, with the accent either on patriotic sentiments (e.g. Glinka's *A Life for the Tsar*) or, coming to our own times, on the richness of a country's folk-lore and the nostalgic attractions of its soil. In the latter category the example of Bartók in Hungary is outstanding.

Today, however, for the majority of contemporary composers conscious nationalism has ceased to be a source of inspiration. Yet was it not Stravinsky himself who said: 'Il faut avoir un passeport'? And in this context the case of another composer, the Italian Dallapiccola, comes to mind. Both are clearly more interested in the intellectual than in the emotional or, indeed, any extra-musical aspects of music; and yet in neither is an element of nationalism altogether absent. Their music is an excellent example of that subtler form of nationalism referred to above, which has its roots in culture and tradition and reveals itself, not in mere mannerisms of style, but in ways of thinking and of expressing thoughts which, although unconscious, are none the less profoundly characteristic of the country and culture to which an artist belongs. And so I think it would be safe to say that, while nationalism is not deliberately cultivated in the works of the major composers in its more external and obvious forms, yet each nation still preserves in varying degree certain idiosyncrasies of style and idiom, still tends to put emphasis on one aspect of music rather than another, and still, perhaps unconsciously, allows the voice of tradition and heredity to make itself heard, if only in discreet undertones. And since this 'stylistic' nationalism, as I have called it, is nowhere more apparent than in the music of France, in the pages that follow traces of it, however unobtrusive, will be found, not only in the majority of the works discussed but also in the general aesthetic and intellectual climate prevailing in all the arts in the period we are considering.

CHAPTER TWO

UNDERCURRENTS OF REVOLT

The break in the continuity of the development of French music in the nineteenth century occurred when the influence of César Franck and the 'school' he had founded and inspired began to wane in the last decade of the century and it became clear that a new spirit was abroad which, by openly dissenting from many of the views and theories hitherto unthinkingly accepted by orthodox musicians, could be seen as a challenge to the musical 'Establishment' of the day. Already composers like Edouard Lalo (1823–1892) and Emmanuel Chabrier (1841–1894) had written works—for example Lalo's *Namouna* and Chabrier's highly unconventional piano pieces and operettas—which belonged to no 'school' and seemed to be the free and unfettered expression of their composers' personalities. And they were not the only ones. As early as 1887 Erik Satie (1866–1925), who, as we shall see, was destined to become a leading figure in the avant-garde of the next century, had startled the musical world with his three Sarabandes whose unconventional and 'advanced' harmonies anticipated the innovations of Debussy and Ravel; and it was only a few years later that an event took place that could be said to mark the opening of a new era in music—the first performance in 1892 of Debussy's *Prélude à l'après-midi d'un Faune*. It was an important and significant event in more ways than one. Not only were the idiom and vocabulary and actual sound of this music unlike anything that the public—even the connoisseurs—had heard before; the very choice of subject and text, taken from the work of the most avant-garde poet of the day, Stéphane Mallarmé (1842–1898), pointed to an unusual awareness on the part of the composer of trends in contemporary literature and an obvious sympathy with the 'Symbolist' aesthetic of which

Mallarmé was, so to speak, the high priest. (I shall be returning to this subject in Chapter 5.)

This was the epoch, too, of a sort of semi-underground or rather marginal anti-Establishment movement in the other arts, typified by such figures as Henri (the 'Douanier') Rousseau in painting, Alfred Jarry and Guillaume Apollinaire in literature and, as we have seen, Erik Satie in music. Though partly a *fin-de-siècle* reaction against the somewhat staid and complacent values of the nineteenth century, it was also the first manifestation of that new 'libertarian' attitude towards the arts (and, indeed, society in general: cf. *Ubu Roi*) which was to be carried still further in the next century, the first two decades of which alone saw the rise and fall of so many intellectual or aesthetic '-isms'—Dadaism, Surrealism, Futurism, Simultanism, Cubism, to mention only a few—all of which, like the Impressionism and Symbolism of the preceding century, affected all the arts in a greater or lesser degree. Moreover, it is undoubtedly to the influence of these 'movements', or at any rate to the kind of climate that engendered them, that we can attribute the paternity of some of the more extreme manifestations of that calculated incoherence in music and the plastic arts especially which today, in ultra-modern circles, passes for emancipation. But now, before attempting to assess the extent to which French music at that time was or was not affected by these various movements, it might be helpful to cast a quick glance at them and recall what their aims were and what they set out to do.

The earliest in date, if we except the cult of Cubism in painting which reached its peak in the period 1908–12, emanated from Italy and was called Futurism. Its founder was Filippo Tommaso Marinetti (1876–1944) whose aim was 'to create the aesthetic of machinery as the master of speed, synthesis, order and the art of living'. The cult of the Machine led to the glorification of railway-stations, factories and steel-foundries and all the noise and turmoil and excitement of urban living— a tendency that was already noticeable in the work of the

Belgian poet Emile Verhaeren—and a reckless determination to wipe out the art of the past. On 20 February 1909 Marinetti published in the Paris newspaper *Le Figaro* his *First Futurist Manifesto*, from which the following quotations are taken:

'A racing motor-car . . . a roaring motor-car which seems to be running on shrapnel is more beautiful than the 'Victory of Samothrace'. . . .

The Past is balsam for prisoners, invalids, men on their death-beds who see the Future closed to them.

We will have none of it. We are young, strong, living—We are *Futurists*.

Museums are cemeteries—public dormitories. . . .

We are out to glorify War—the only health-giver of the world.

We extol aggressive movement, feverish insomnia, the somer-sault, the box on the ear. . . .

Poetry must be a violent onslaught. There is no masterpiece without aggressiveness. . . .

We shall sing of . . . the nocturnal vibration of arsenals and workshops beneath their electric moons; of factories suspended from the clouds by strings of smoke; of broad-chested loco-motives galloping on rails . . . of aeroplanes with propellors whose sound is like the flapping of flags and the cheers of a roaring crowd.

It is from Italy that we launch this Manifesto of Destructive Incendiary Violence.

Italy has been too long the market-place of the second-hand Art Trade.

On then, Good Incendiaries! Fire the libraries! Turn the floods into the museums! Let the famous picture float! We cast our challenge to the stars!'[1]

Marinetti also dreamed of a language of 'mots en liberté'

[1] R. H. Wilenski, from whose *Modern French Painters* the above extracts are quoted, also records that Mussolini at one time came under the in-fluence of Marinetti who, he said, 'instilled in me the feeling of the ocean and the power of the machine'.

which would rival the noises and confusion of modern cities—
an idea which was later to be exploited by the founder of the
Simultanist movement (Henri-Martin Barzun), who imagined
all the noises of the world being mixed with words of individual and collective speech, and in 1917 actually organised a
'Simultanist session' at the Théâtre des Champs-Elysées in
Paris. The demonstration, however, was a failure owing to the
impossibility of distinguishing words in a confusion of syn-
thesised voices.[1]

Futurism found its first adherents among writers and
painters; among the latter, artists like Severini and Boccioni
achieved a certain notoriety, although attempts to apply to
painting the technique of the cinema in order to suggest over-
lapping and fragmented motion—e.g. the successive steps of a
dance—on a plane surface were not really convincing. It was
not until later that an attempt was made to apply the principles
of Futurism to music; but although, here, again, nothing of
any value was accomplished, the theories of Luigi Russolo and
Balilla Pratella which led to the creation of an orchestra of
Bruiteurs, or noise-making machines, are worth mentioning if
only because they can be considered as the first deliberate
attempt to break down the barriers between music and noise,
thus anticipating the invention, half a century later, of what we
call today *Musique concrète* and the willingness shown by certain
contemporary composers to look upon noise as a legitimate
extension of the vocabulary of music.

It was in 1913 that Russolo drew up his Manifesto on *The
Art of Noises* in the form of a letter to 'My dear Balilla Pratella,

---

[1] The following definition of a *poème simultané*, of which 'the subject is
the value of the human voice', was given by Hugo Ball, one of the
founders of 'Dada' (see p. 18): 'The vocal organ represents the Individual Soul as it wanders flanked by supernatural companions. The
noises represent the inarticulate, inexorable and ultimately derisive forces
which constitute the background. The poem carries the message that mankind is swallowed up in a mechanistic process. In a generalised and com-
pressed form, it represents the battle of the human voice against a world
which menaces, ensnares and finally destroys it, a world whose rhythm
and whose din are inescapable.'

great Futurist composer', informing him that it was 'while I was listening to the orchestral performance of your overwhelming MUSICA FUTURISTA there came to my mind the idea of a new art: the Art of Noises, a logical consequence of your marvellous innovations.'

Then followed a lengthy review of how music developed through the ages, 'passing from the perfect consonance, with a few passing dissonances, to the complicated and persistent dissonances which characterise the music of today.... This musical evolution parallels the growing multiplicity of machines, which everywhere are assisting mankind ... creating so many varieties and combinations of noise that pure musical sound—with its poverty and monotony—no longer awakes any emotion in the hearer.... We must break out of this narrow circle of pure musical sounds and conquer the infinite variety of noise-sounds.... We Futurists have all deeply loved the music of the great composers; Beethoven and Wagner for many years wrung our hearts. But now we are satiated with them, and derive much greater pleasure from ideally combining the noises of street-cars, internal-combustion engines, automobiles and busy crowds than from rehearing, for example the *Eroica* or the *Pastorale*. We cannot see the immense apparatus of the modern orchestra without being profoundly disappointed by its feeble acoustic achievements. ... Let us enter, as Futurists, one of these institutions for musical anaemia (a concert-hall). The first measure assails your ear with the boredom of the already-heard, and causes you to anticipate the boredom of the measure to come ... while we await an unusual emotion that never arrives.... Away! let us be gone, since we shall not much longer succeed in restraining a desire to create a new musical realism by a generous distribution of sonorous blows and slaps leaping nimbly over violins, pianofortes, contrebasses and groaning organs.[1] Away! ... let

---

[1] An intelligent anticipation of the kind of physical misuse to which musical instruments today are being subjected by certain musical exhibitionists in 'advanced' circles.

us wander through a great modern city with our ears more attentive than our eyes, and distinguish the sound of water, air or gas in metal pipes; the purring of motors (which breathe and pulsate with an indubitable animalism), the throbbing of valves, the pounding of pistons, the screeching of gears, the clatter of street-cars on their rails, the cracking of whips, the flapping of awnings and flags. We shall amuse ourselves by orchestrating in our minds the noise of metal shutters of store windows, the slamming of doors, the bustle and shuffle of crowds, the multitudinous uproar of rail-road stations, forges, mills, printing presses, power stations and underground railways. Nor should the new noises of modern warfare be forgotten. Recently the poet Marinetti, in a letter from the trenches of Adrianopolis, described to me in admirably unfettered language the orchestra of a great battle.' Then follows an extraordinary evocation of a battlefield expressed in onomatopaeic terms, and the Manifesto concludes with an appeal to 'young musicians of genius and audacity to listen attentively to all noises, so that they may understand the varied rhythms of which they are composed, their principal tone and their secondary tones. . . . Out of this will come not merely an understanding of noises, but even a taste and an enthusiasm for them. Our increased perceptivity, which has already acquired futurist eyes will then have futurist ears. . . . I submit these statements, my dear Pratella, to your futuristic genius. . . . I am not a professional musician, and therefore have no acoustic prejudices and no works to defend. I am a futurist painter projecting into an art he loves and has studied his desire to renovate all things. Being therefore more audacious than a professional musician could be and convinced that audacity makes all things lawful and all things possible, I have imagined a great renovation of music through the Art of Noises.' (Milan, 11 March 1913.)

What in fact emerged from all this verbiage on the practical side was the formation of an orchestra of noise-machines, or *Bruiteurs*, consisting of the following instruments:

Thunderclappers, Crashers, Splashers, Bellowers, Whistlers, Hissers, Snorers, Whisperers, Mutterers, Bustlers, Gurglers, Screamers, Screechers, Buzzers, Cracklers, Shriekers, Howlers, Wheezers, etc. However the concert organised in Paris in 1921 to illustrate Russolo's theories and exhibit his new 'orchestra' fell very flat—partly, no doubt, because all the instruments, despite their exciting and suggestive names, sounded very much alike, but chiefly, of course, because the whole idea was devoid of any artistic significance. Nevertheless the Manifesto is worth recalling because it is symbolic of the same kind of morbid craving for novelty at any price that is so prevalent today in the arts; and it is important to bear in mind that beneath the apparently unruffled surface of the main stream of creative art—music, painting and literature—in Europe even before the 1914 war, these subversive undercurrents were already making themselves felt.

The next 'movement' of a comparable nature, but which had wider repercussions and lasted longer than Futurism, was launched during the 1914 war. How 'Dada' was born and what its aims were has often been recounted; but the story of its rise and fall may not be familiar to every student today and so may briefly be outlined here to complete our picture of the various disruptive movements whose aim was the destruction of orthodoxy in the arts during the early part of this century. As much of this comedy was played out in France, such influence as it may or may not have had on French music during this period is a question that has to be considered, even though the answer in this case is very little. There was no Dadaist composer, though there is evidence that some members of the French group 'Les Six', as well as Erik Satie, Stravinsky and even Hindemith, did write music for certain Dadaist manifestations.

Dada came to Paris in 1919 from Zürich *via* New York and Germany. Its founders were the Rumanian writer Tristan Tzara, the Alsatian artist Hans Arp, and a German writer and producer called Hugo Ball. The origin of the name Dada has never been definitely settled, but it is generally accepted (on the authority of Arp) that it was discovered or invented by Tristan Tzara on 8 February 1916 at six o'clock in the evening at the Café de la Terrasse in Zürich. In French the word means 'hobby-horse'; and according to the legend, Tzara hit upon it by opening a dictionary at random and pin-pointing the word. (According to Ball, however, he himself suggested the name after listening to Tzara and another Rumanian talking, their conversation being punctuated by frequent 'Da, da's', meaning 'Yes, yes'.) In any event it was immediately adopted as their slogan by a group of Continental artists who had come to Switzerland to escape the war and to launch an anti-art movement as a protest against the slaughter and destruction that was taking place all over Europe. The movement, in fact, was expressive of the same kind of revolt as that seen in recent years among opponents of the war in Viet-Nam, though it was confined to avant-garde intellectual and artistic circles, and the public played no part in it at all, except to display their hostility. Gradually it claimed more and more adherents, published more and more manifestoes and organised more and more exhibitions and manifestations both in Europe and America designed exclusively to provoke and shock the bourgeois public, and to create a state of complete nihilism in the domain of literature and the arts. Dada stood for the abolition of all accepted values, and admitted that its object was to 'spit in the eye of the world'. It set out to reduce everything to nonsense. It was anti-art and anti-life and anti-society and anti-everything else. It was even anti-Dada—for the slogan that heralded the appearance of the first *Dada Bulletin* was 'All true Dadas are anti-Dada.'

Dada's reign in France was a short one, lasting barely three years; and by 1922 it had fizzled out to be succeeded, however, under the leadership of the late André Breton, one of its most active members, by Surrealism, a much more positive aesthetic creed based on the conscious exploitation of the unconscious. The organ of the new movement was *La Révolution Surréaliste*, and unlike Dada, Surrealism had come to stay; indeed, its force is not yet spent, and its influence can be felt in much of modern art. The word itself, it is worth noting, was first used by Guillaume Apollinaire who referred, in a programme note he had written for the ballet *Parade* (produced by Diaghilev in 1917 with the collaboration of Cocteau, Picasso and Satie)' . . . a sort of sur-realism in which I see the point of departure for a series of manifestations of that New Spirit which promises to modify the arts and the conduct of life (*mœurs*) from top to bottom in a universal joyousness'.

The involvement of French artists in all these movements and undercurrents that marked the first two decades of the twentieth century is something that has to be borne in mind when setting the scene for a survey of the evolution of French music during this period; and it is for this reason that I have outlined in some detail the nature and aims of the most important of these movements in order to show that the whole period was far from stable. After the second world war the climate altered again, and other influences made themselves felt which will be considered in a later chapter.

CHAPTER THREE

THE NEW 'OLD MASTERS':
GABRIEL FAURÉ AND VINCENT D'INDY

1900: 'la Belle Epoque'! The opening years of the new century were for the French bourgeoisie, enjoying the first-fruits of the industrial revolution, a period of prosperity, carefree and impregnated with an atmosphere of luxury and good living. This was the heyday of the boulevardier and the cocotte, driving in the Bois in the mornings in their handsome *équipages*, taking their apéritifs on the Grands Boulevards at the Café Napolitain, and wining and dining *chez Maxim*. Montmartre was still the centre of Bohemian life, and many artists had their studios on the *Butte* and frequented cabarets like *Le Chat Noir*, *L'Auberge du Clou*, *La Nouvelle Athènes* and the famous *Lapin Agile*,[1] or dropped in at the *Moulin Rouge* to watch the *cancan* and the artists made famous by Toulouse-Lautrec until his death in 1901.

The Dreyfus *affaire*, which had been splitting the nation into two irreconcilable factions and had had many literary as well as social repercussions, was still a controversial topic, and the growing division between Left and Right culminated in the emergence of Jaurès as leader of the new Socialist movement and the creation by the Right-wing extremist, Charles Maurras, of his Royalist *Action Française* group, whose aim was the establishment of a dictatorial monarchist régime—a policy which he continued to preach right up till the second world war, after which he was arrested as a collaborator and died while awaiting trial at the age of eighty-four.

[1] A corruption of: 'Le Lapin à Gill'—Gill being the name of the artist who had painted the rabbit on the front door of what had once been his house.

But 1900 was also the year of the Great Exhibition which made Paris the centre of attraction in Europe for countless thousands of tourists from all over the world; and, coinciding with the Exhibition, there took place in the Grand Palais on the Champs-Elysées, specially built for the occasion, the first big exhibition of Impressionist painters, showing the work of Monet, Sisley, Degas, Renoir, Pissarro, Manet, etc., who, after being looked down on and ridiculed for so long, were at last receiving the recognition they deserved.

In the world of music, meantime, the big names were still (in 1900) Saint-Saëns, Massenet, Fauré and d'Indy; for Debussy and Ravel, representing the avant-garde, had not yet revealed their full stature, although it was already abundantly clear to all discerning critics that, with *L'Après-midi d'un Faune*, *Nocturnes* and the String Quartet, the young Debussy, at least, was emerging as a new voice in music that would have to be reckoned with, even though he had not yet revealed his full stature as the composer of *Pelléas et Mélisande*, which was not to have its historic first performance until 1902. Nevertheless, although the four composers I mentioned at the beginning of this paragraph all belonged in a sense to the nineteenth century, two of them at least lived to be prominent and important figures in French music well into the twentieth. And yet, although all of them, with the exception of Massenet who died in 1912, actually out-lived Debussy, we still think of the latter as being more essentially a twentieth-century composer than any of those I have named could claim to be. This is because Debussy is now seen to have had more influence on developments in the music of this century than any of his contemporaries, and to have been, in fact, the 'founding father', no less, of what we now call 'modern music'. I therefore propose to consider the *cas Debussy* in separate chapters, but before doing so to give some account of two of the composers I have mentioned who in different ways made an important contribution to the music of our time, and helped to establish France as the most important country, musically, in Europe at the beginning of this century. As neither Saint-Saëns nor Massenet quite come into this category and, in any case, had written almost all the major works on which their reputation depends before the turn of the century, this leaves us with d'Indy and Fauré as the two most important 'transitional' composers who were still, in the new century, whatever the younger men were doing, very much the representatives of French music in the eyes of the world right up to and even after the 1914 war. The reputation and importance of Gabriel Fauré (1845–1924) are so firmly established and recognised and his works on the whole so much better known and appreciated abroad than those of many of his contemporaries that he has come to be considered as perhaps in some ways the most representative French composer of his generation. He was also, in his own unobtrusive way a pioneer, enriching and enlarging, in a way that points the meaning of the saying about art concealing art, the harmonic language of his day and, like a musical John the Baptist, preparing the way, in the words of one of his younger contemporaries, 'for the great revelation brought about by Debussy'.

Unlike almost all other French composers of his period, Fauré was never a pupil of the Paris Conservatoire, although in later life he became its Director. He was trained in the school of Abraham Louis Niedermeyer (1802–1861), the Swiss composer and pedagogue who founded, in 1835, the *Ecole de musique classique et religieuse*. Here he received a thorough and liberal musical education, and came for a time under the influence of Saint-Saëns who as a young man had joined the teaching staff of the *Ecole* when Fauré was a boy of fifteen; and it was through Saint-Saëns that he first became acquainted with the music of Wagner. However, although, like so many of his contemporaries, he went in 1878 and again the following year to Germany to hear the *Ring* and was duly impressed (as indeed were all French composers of his generation), he was one of the few who never, even temporarily, allowed himself to come under Wagner's 'influence'. Fortunately, however, Saint-Saëns, though only ten years older than his pupil at that time, already had a wide knowledge of music, and was always ready to share his enthusiasms with his pupils. Thus the young Fauré had every opportunity of listening to and learning about music of all kinds from Bach to Liszt, and found in Saint-Saëns a teacher who was always ready to encourage his own first essays at composition. The friendship thus formed turned out to be a lifelong one.

Gabriel-Urbain Fauré was born on 12 May 1845 in the small town of Pamiers, not far from Carcassonne, in the Ariège *département* in southern France. His father, Toussaint-Honoré Fauré, was a village school-master who rose to become the director of a teachers' training college in the locality. His youngest son's musical gifts do not seem to have been in any way inherited; they were first discovered when he was heard, while still a small boy, improvising on the harmonium in the village church; and it was this that led to his being sent to study with Niedermeyer, who had already founded a society for the performance of generally unknown or neglected church music of the sixteenth and seventeenth centuries before opening in Paris his *Ecole*, where the young Fauré went to study at the age of nine. Eleven years later he obtained his first professional appointment, that of organist at a church at Rennes in Brittany. During the next ten years, during which his professional career was interrupted by a period of military service during the Franco-Prussian war, his musical activities were mainly in the organ-lofts of various churches in and around Paris, culminating in his appointment, after assisting Widor at Saint-Sulpice, as *maître de chapelle* at the Madeleine, where Saint-Saëns had just resigned his post as organist in favour of Théodore Dubois.

After his engagement to the singer Marianne Viardot, daughter of Pauline Viardot-Garcia, had been broken off, he eventually married, six years later, the daughter of a celebrated sculptor, Marie Frémiet, who apparently took little or no part in her husband's musical career, but presented him with two sons and provided him with a secure and comfortable domestic background.

He was over thirty before he published any composition of importance (the first Violin Sonata and the C minor Piano Quartet date from this period); and it was not until he was forty-one that his genius found its fullest expression (and public recognition) in the Requiem Mass he composed in 1886 in memory of his father. Ten years later Fauré was appointed chief organist at the Madeleine and professor of composition at the Paris Conservatoire, after having composed some of his best-known works: the song-cycle *La Bonne Chanson*, the second Piano Quartet and the *Pavane* for orchestra. His class at the Conservatoire, where he acted more in an 'advisory' than in a strictly professorial capacity, included some of the most distinguished names in French music: Maurice Ravel, Florent Schmitt, Roger-Ducasse, Louis Aubert, Charles Koechlin, Gabriel Grovlez and Nadia Boulanger.

In 1898 Fauré went to London for the production of Maeterlinck's *Pelléas et Mélisande*, for which he had written the incidental music, at the Prince of Wales's Theatre, with Martin Harvey and Mrs. Patrick Campbell in the title roles. Two years later another important commission resulted in the production, in 1900, in the open-air amphitheatre at Béziers, of Jean Lorrain and Ferdinand Hérold's *Prométhée* (an adaptation of the classic legend of Prometheus) for which Fauré provided orchestral and choral incidental music. He was now beginning to be recognised for what he was, a composer of real distinction who was widely admired and respected, so that, in liberal circles at least, his appointment in 1905 as Director of the Conservatoire was warmly welcomed. A few years later his official career was crowned by his nomination to membership of the Institut de France.

As Head of the Paris Conservatoire Fauré was faced with the task of breathing new life, so to speak, into this august body, which had sunk to a very low ebb under its previous Director, Théodore Dubois (1837–1924), a highly reactionary and old-fashioned type of academic musician who had brought about his own downfall largely through his persistent persecution of one of his most distinguished students—Maurice Ravel. After being placed second in the *Prix de Rome* competition in 1901, Ravel failed to gain a place at all the next two years and in 1905 was not even allowed to sit for the examination. Such high-handed and insensitive treatment of a man of thirty who was already famous as the composer of such masterpieces as the String Quartet, the piano piece *Jeux d'eau* and the *Shéhérazade* song-cycle, shocked the musical world, and what came to be known as *l'affaire Ravel* was soon being discussed in the highest circles. The matter came to a head when Romain Rolland, the eminent writer and musicologist, finally referred it to the Ministry of Fine Arts, with the result that Dubois was forced to resign and Fauré was appointed his successor on the under-standing that he would carry out necessary and long overdue reforms.

The Paris Conservatoire de Musique was established by the Convention in 1795, having been preceded by the *Ecole Royale de Chant* which opened under François-Joseph Gossec (1734–1829), the Belgian composer, in 1784. Bernard Sarrette (1765–1858) was the Conservatoire's first Director, and on his retire-ment in 1822 he was succeeded by Cherubini (1760–1842) who during the twenty years of his administration placed the new establishment on a firm foundation and added greatly to its prestige.

Daniel François Auber (1782–1871), the operatic composer, was Director for the next thirty years; and after him came Ambroise Thomas (1811–1896) whose successor was Théodore Dubois (1837–1924) who, as we have seen, was invited to retire in favour of Fauré.

The trouble with the Paris Conservatoire during most of the nineteenth century, after Cherubini's lengthy and on the whole enlightened administration, was that it tended to be more of a training college for executants, with the accent heavily on singers—and operatic singers at that—rather than a school where pupils could receive an all-round musical education embracing the history and theory of music as well as learning to play an instrument or sing showy arias from operas, often without knowing anything about their context or dramatic significance. Chamber music was neglected, so was the art of lieder singing. The teaching, in fact, tended to be directed towards the single goal of obtaining as many prizes as possible, and too little attention was paid to the intrinsic value of the kind of music which singer and instrumentalists were encouraged to learn in order to show off their technical proficiency. As to composition, the *Prix de Rome*, which was instituted by Sarrette in 1803 and much coveted as it entitled the laureate to spend three years in Rome at the expense of the French government (besides being a useful testimonial for the job-seeker beginning his professional career) was the highest recompense any student could obtain in this field. Yet the number of *Prix de Rome* winners who later turned out to be anything but mediocrities could almost be counted on the fingers of one hand. The judges were usually highly conservative, not to say reactionary musical pedants, and this meant that a really gifted student with an original turn of mind stood very little chance of winning the Prize. Exceptions were Debussy in 1884, and before him Berlioz, Gounod, Bizet and Massenet. Since 1900 there have been perhaps not more than four well-known names among the prize-winners—those of Florent Schmitt, André Caplet (Debussy's great friend and interpreter), Lily Boulanger and the contemporary composer Henri Dutilleux. The vast majority of *Prix de Rome* winners were never heard of again; but among those who either failed or never troubled to compete we find such distinguished names as César Franck, Vincent d'Indy, Camille Saint-Saëns, Edouard Lalo, Emmanuel Chabrier, Ernest Chausson, Albert Roussel—and, of course, Gabriel Fauré who now found himself nevertheless at the head of the august establishment in the Faubourg Poissonière (now 14 rue de Madrid). The reason reported to have been given by Dubois to explain his distrust of

Fauré, namely that 'he was transforming the Conservatoire in-to a temple for the music of the future' is typical of the reactionary attitude of so many of Fauré's predecessors; and it is significant that it took a scandal like that of *l'affaire Ravel* to make those in high places realise that the time had come for sweeping reforms in what was, after all, one of France's most famous educational and cultural institutions. For it is only fair to remember that it had in the past attracted to its staff many distinguished musicians—for example Fétis, the musicologist and Reicha who taught Berlioz—while since Fauré's time it has become increasingly modernised so that today we find on its teaching staff respected names like that of Nadia Boulanger, for example, and even avant-garde composers such as Milhaud and Messiaen. Teaching standards are high, and the outlook in all departments far more liberal and progressive than it used to be.

Fauré remained as Head of the Conservatoire for fifteen years; but in 1920 he was forced to resign as the deafness from which he had suffered for many years now made it impossible for him to stay in office. Yet during those twenty years he had been composing some of his finest works; and in the four years that still remained to him he composed the second Piano Quintet and his only String Quartet which he had only just time to finish before he died on 4 November 1924.

Although Fauré lived the greater part of his life in the nine-teenth century, we are nevertheless considering him here primarily as a twentieth-century composer if only to discover the extent, if any, to which he could be said to have 'influenced' later developments in French music. Looking at his work as a whole it becomes clear that perhaps his greatest claim to be considered as in any sense a pioneer rests mainly on his extraordinarily subtle harmonic sensitivity which enabled him to invest almost everything he wrote with unexpected over- and undertones which give to his music a peculiar flavour that both charms and intrigues the ear. A fondness for incessant modulations and enharmonic surprise transitions characterises all Fauré's music; as well as a kind of restless mobility, often taking the form of widespread arpeggios concealing within them all kinds of subtle and surprising harmonic changes. And all this is done with no desire to shock or astonish; often it is only on closer examination that some startlingly original progression or harmonic twist is revealed that on first hearing might almost have passed un-noticed. While his art in general was classic in its emotional discretion and avoidance of false emphasis of any kind, and its invariably polished and impeccable craftsmanship, it was never in the slightest degree academic. On the contrary; in his discreetly daring harmonic innovations he was, in fact, a pioneer. But he had his own ideas about how to make a revolution in music, and it is typical of the man and his methods that he succeeded in making one almost without letting anyone know what he was doing. Yet to speak of Fauré's 'influence' on twentieth-century French music would scarcely be correct. His was a highly personal mode of expression which, though universally admired, was yet very much the reflection of a temperament and an artistic sensibility more concerned with expressing itself than with any conscious desire to extend the vocabulary of music in accordance with some preconceived theory. As to Fauré's reputation outside France, the tendency has always been to under-rate him—for reasons which, as Mr. Norman Suckling in his admirable study of the composer[1] has pointed out, usually stem from 'a misapprehension that goes very deeply into the psychology of art, for it is due ultimately to the false value so often set on strenuousness, as such. From this error, partly romantic and partly what Matthew Arnold would have called Hebraic, derived in great part the fortunes of German music in the nineteenth century; through accepting it, not only in this country but in some departments of French musical life itself, it became possible to identify 'depth' in art with those uneasy stirrings which so often are nothing but

---

[1] *Fauré* ('Master Musicians' series, J. M. Dent, London 1946).

turgidity, and to treat as superficial the 'Olympian' serenity of those artists who had, as it were, no need to "wrestle with the angel" (as Brahms expressed it), but had him at their service from the first.'

The same author, with reference to what he calls Fauré's characteristic Hellenic quality of 'rational serenity' also quotes a phrase used by Charles Maurras in speaking of the ancient Athenians: 'Feeling was the spring of all their behaviour, and it was reason that they set upon their altar. The event is the greatest in the history of the world.' And he goes on, in a final summing up of Fauré's achievement, to declare that his music 'aristocratic in its disdain to compete for favour, Hellenic in the splendid finality of its resolution of material into form, is worthy of a place among the greatest masterpieces because it offers none but the most genuine credentials for admission to their company'.

With this judgment as a general recognition of Fauré's outstanding qualities it is difficult to disagree, although one may feel it could perhaps bear a little scaling down. Though a good deal more than a *petit maître*, Fauré's place is scarcely among the giants. There is an analogy with Schumann which should not, however, be pressed too far (Fauré could not have written the symphonies and other large-scale works) but which is valid so far as the songs and the piano and chamber-music are concerned. The best of Fauré's mélodies will indeed bear comparison with the best of Schumann's Lieder; one has only to think of the matchless setting of Verlaine's *Clair de lune* and such gems as *Après un rêve*, *Lydia*, *Le secret*, *Les berceaux*, *Le parfum impérissable*, and the big song-cycles *La bonne chanson* and *L'Horizon chimérique*, to realise that these exquisite songs, in which a perfect fusion between poetic content and musical expression is achieved by the subtlest means, are indeed the work of a master.

An intelligent tribute to just this aspect of Fauré's art as a song-writer was paid by the French musicologist, the late Jean Chantavoine, in his obituary article in *Le Ménéstrel* of

14 November 1924 (quoted by Mr. Norman Suckling (op. cit.) which I think is worth reproducing here. Speaking of Fauré's affinities with 'Parnassian' and 'Symbolist' poets like Leconte de Lisle, Sully-Prud'homme, Albert Samain and Verlaine, Chantavoine makes this interesting point: 'It is not enough to say that he was their *interpreter*, nor even their *complement*. . . . In some cases he has actually *revealed* them by opening up for them that region of our minds which the choicest words in poetic speech have otherwise failed to penetrate. . . . In this respect Gabriel Fauré (together with Henri Duparc) played, in the Parnassian and Symbolist age of France, a part recalling that of Schumann in the romantic age in Germany; on this account he belongs henceforth, not merely to the history of French music, but to that of French poetry and French artistic sensibility.' This raises the whole question of the relations between music and literature generally, and between certain composers and writers more specifically, which is of prime importance when considering developments in French music at the beginning of this century; and I propose to deal with this subject in a later chapter.

Turning now to another domain to which Fauré made in some ways his most memorable contribution—namely, that of chamber-music and works for piano solo, we find again the same consistently high level of both inspiration and craftsmanship. The two pairs of quartets and quintets with piano contain some of his best music and are outstanding examples of modern French chamber-music at its best, only equalled, if not surpassed, by the nobly serene and austere String Quartet which was the last work Fauré completed before his death.

As to the piano music, since it forms, after all, one of the most important parts of the composer's total output, it is as good an approach as any other to the study of his genius. In it there will be found that same absence of rhetoric and writing for effect, that restraint and delicacy of touch which characterise the *Requiem* and the bulk of his orchestral and chamber works; and we shall find, too, something of the lyrical beauty and intimate expressiveness of the songs, the best of which, as we have seen, are among the most perfect examples of Fauré's art.

It is perhaps significant that in his compositions for piano solo Fauré adopted the forms and titles we associate especially with Chopin. Thus there are thirteen Nocturnes, thirteen Barcarolles, six Impromptus, nine Preludes, a Ballade and four Valses-Caprices. He wrote no sonata for the piano, but the Theme and Variations in C sharp minor is a major work, not without a certain resemblance to Schumann's *Études symphoniques*. Most of the piano works contain treasures of harmonic subtleties and melodic felicities, and some of them music of a very high order. The boldness and originality of certain harmonic progressions and those surprising modulations which Fauré handled with such consummate skill, and yet so unobtrusively, cannot fail to strike the hearer. There are examples on almost every page. Yet it is important to remember, as Fauré's English biographer has pointed out, that his innovations were mainly in the *syntax* and not the *vocabulary* of musical language. He did not invent new chords or experiment, except to a very limited extent, with new modes or scales; but he did manipulate with extraordinary ingenuity the accepted harmonic language of his day, and delighted in discovering new ways of travelling from one tonality to another, taking full advantage of the possibilities offered by enharmonic transitions of which he was particularly fond. If his piano writing can be faulted, a point for criticism would be a certain 'fussiness', an impression of being 'over-dressed' due to the elaborate and restless figuration in which he tended to clothe his themes, sometimes to an extent which makes it difficult, as it were, to see the wood for the trees. It is this feature, perhaps more than any other, that distinguishes the piano works of Fauré, important landmarks though they are in the annals of French music, from those of Chopin on the one hand where, however elaborate the ornamentation, the outline is never obscured, and of Debussy on the other, whose keyboard writing, with its carefully spaced chords, giving his harmonies time to breathe and vibrate, and general absence of figuration, opened up a new era in piano technique, and showed a more profound understanding of the resources of the instrument than that of any other composer before or since. Yet even if Fauré's pianistic style may not always be flawless, nothing can detract from the profound musicality of his inspiration and the beauty and elegance with which his ideas are invariably expressed.

We have had occasion to refer to the essentially classical and 'Hellenic' nature of Fauré's art in general which naturally inclined him to choose, in the only two operatic ventures he allowed himself, a classical Greek subject; but neither his *Prométhée* (1900—libretto by F. A. Hérold after Aeschylus) nor his *Pénélope* (1913—libretto by René Fauchois after Homer) can really be said to be representative of his genius, though both works contain some fine music. Curiously enough he had no real feeling for the orchestra, and was even often content to leave the orchestration of his scores to others; thus the second act of *Pénélope* is said to have been scored by Dukas, d'Indy and Cortot; while the orchestration of *Prométhée*, which was first produced in the open-air theatre at Béziers, was entrusted by the composer to a local musician in charge of a regimental band. In a work like the *Requiem*, however, from which all dramatic emphasis is rigidly excluded, and the customary 'Dies irae' section even omitted altogether to emphasise the work's essentially serene and contemplative nature and its author's instinctive and characteristic repudiation of the notion of a vindictive deity, Fauré employs only a modest orchestra which is treated more like a chamber-music ensemble. This quiet and gentle work is the one by which he is perhaps most widely known; and it has at least the distinction of being free from most of the faults which had tended to debase most of the French nineteenth-century religious music perpetrated by his predecessors.

It is hardly necessary today to stress the importance of

Gabriel Fauré as a key figure in the French musical renaissance that came in with the twentieth century, and put France definitely on the musical map of Europe from which she had been too long excluded. But Fauré was not the only French composer to bring about this revaluation of his country's claims to parity with other nations in the musical field; and we must now consider the case of one of his most distinguished contemporaries, in the person of a young French nobleman, the Vicomte Paul Marie Théodore Vincent d'Indy, who was born in 1851, and was thus Fauré's junior by some six years. He came from an old established aristocratic and Catholic family, and during his childhood and youth was largely brought up and guided by his paternal grandmother who instilled in him a high standard of moral and intellectual discipline. This influence remained with him all his life, and was no doubt responsible for the somewhat austere and forbidding character of much of his music which his detractors were rather inclined to exaggerate, while shutting their eyes to the obvious beauties and spontaneity of his best works, such as, for example, the *Symphonie sur un chant montagnard français* (*Symphonie Cévenole*) directly inspired by the folk music and scenery of his native Cévennes, the district in southern France where he had his ancestral home and where he wrote some of his best music.

Unlike Fauré, who was a product of the Niedermeyer school, d'Indy had come early under the influence of the Franco-Belgian César Franck who in the latter part of the nineteenth century had gathered round him a group of devoted disciples who had learned from him to venerate the great masters of the past, notably Bach, Beethoven and Palestrina, together with Gregorian plainsong and the music of Richard Wagner. After Franck's death, three of his old pupils, d'Indy, Charles Bordes and Alexandre Guilmant, founded in Paris in 1894 the *Schola Cantorum* to perpetuate their master's memory and to promote his teaching and ideals. In due course d'Indy became Director of the *Schola* which, with its emphasis on scholarship rather than virtuosity, soon became a serious rival to the official Conservatoire, and began to attract students from all over the world who knew they would find at the *Schola* teaching of a very high order and a thorough training in every branch of music, both practical and theoretical. Standards were high, and the moral and intellectual tone of the school somewhat austere; but what it had to offer to the serious musician was more rewarding and more lasting than the mere acquisition of prizes and diplomas, for to have been a student at the *Schola* was a distinction in itself.

D'Indy, then, had early been imbued with César Franck's veneration for the great German classics, and a tour of the Germanic countries he undertook as a young man in his early twenties enabled him not only to hear a great deal of German music old and new, but to meet some of the greatest musicians of the day, including Brahms and Liszt. A few years later, in 1876, he went to Bayreuth to hear Wagner's *Ring* in the newly opened theatre there, and came back a convinced and fervent Wagnerite. From now on he was obsessed with the idea of renovating French opera in accordance with Wagner's theories which gave him ample intellectual justification for his instinctive antipathy towards the conventional French operatic tradition of the day as exemplified by Meyerbeer, Saint-Saëns and Massenet. At the same time he remembered what Wagner had said about the desirability for French composers, while conforming to the general principles of Wagnerian music-drama, to draw on the literary, historical and folk resources of their own country if they wished to create a truly national opera. The result was, after some years of hard work and thought, a full-length opera in a Prologue and three acts entitled *Fervaal* which had its first performance in 1897. The theme of the opera is the triumph of Christian over pagan ideals and beliefs, the hero Fervaal being a kind of Celtic Parsifal whose mission it is to save his country from the invading Saracens, but only on condition that he remains 'pure' and renounces the love of women. Unable to keep his vows when confronted by Guilhen, the beautiful daughter of the Saracen chief, he confesses his fault to his Druid master and teacher, Arfagard, who tells him he has forfeited the right to command the Celtic army and must die. Fervaal nevertheless leads his troops into battle, but is defeated. He is prepared to die, when suddenly he hears the voice of Guilhen calling him. She is lost on the mountain-side in the snow and Fervaal goes out to rescue her, after killing Arfagard who tries to prevent him. Guilhen dies, and the opera ends with Fervaal climbing the mountain, with Guilhen in his arms, marching towards the 'new' fatherland he sees in a vision—'jeune amour vainqueur de la mort'—and gradually fading into the clouds upon the mountain-top. Despite its somewhat confused mythology, the opera can be seen as a vehicle for the composer's ideas on life and death and art, while the possibilities the story offers for a Wagnerian type of treatment are obvious. Nevertheless, the music startled the critics and the public at the time by its richness and complexity and striking originality, and made a great impression both at its first performance in Brussels in 1897 and in Paris, at the Opéra-Comique, the following year.

Other works in which the influence of Wagner is noticeable were the symphonic poem, or 'légende dramatique' as it was called, *Le chant de la cloche* (based on Schiller's poem *Das Lied von der Glocke*) and two more operas in which the composer was again his own librettist: *L'Etranger*, completed in 1901 and *La légende de Saint Christophe* (composed 1915, produced 1920).

In *L'Etranger*, a small seaside village receives the visit of a mysterious stranger who is regarded with suspicion by the villagers in general, but arouses the interest and sympathy of a young girl, Vita, who tries to persuade him to stay, despite the hostility of the people. 'Je suis celui qui aime, qui rêve', he tells her—'dreaming only of the happiness of all men who are my brothers'. When the time comes for the Stranger to leave, he gives Vita the emerald he was wearing, which had greatly intrigued the villagers, but when he has gone, she throws it into the sea. A violent storm breaks, endangering the lives of the fishermen out at sea. No one attempts to help them until the Stranger reappears and rows out to rescue them, accompanied only by Vita. A huge wave engulfs them, and they are drowned, whereupon the villagers kneel down and sing a De profundis. The allegory here is plain, the Stranger representing the Saviour of humanity.

D'Indy's last opera, on the St. Christopher legend, is an extraordinary patchwork, by no means devoid of musical interest, of moral, political and artistic theories and prejudices: a kind of manifesto attacking the anti-clericalism of the Third Republic and excessive Jewish influence in high places (d'Indy's anti-Semitism was notorious), and making fun of the latest tendencies in French music as represented by Ravel and 'Les Six'. In the words of d'Indy's biographer, Léon Vallas, the work was 'a strange mixture of piety and hatred, of Christianity and paganism, to which d'Indy had committed himself in order to proclaim his Roman Catholic faith and his convictions as a citizen. . . . It was not an opera so much as a compromise between the medieval mystery plays and Wagnerian music-drama. . . . The music is no less disconcerting: a vast synthesis of all the forms, all the styles and all the procedures of technique, declamation and orchestration . . . certain keys are reserved for the expression of certain sentiments and situations, and the general progress of the score as a whole is from B minor at the opening to B major at the close. The orchestration, which is full of original devices, has an airy lightness and a fluid texture more remote than ever from Wagnerian stuffiness. *La Légende de Saint-Christophe*, an ambitious declaration of a faith capable of moving mountains, the noble synthesis, or the ponderous summing-up of an intransigent and wilful artist, is the culmination of an over-idealized art, the exhaustion of a too disdainful manner, magnificent and almost superhuman, the apex of thoughts and expressions inaccessible to the general public.'

If d'Indy were to be judged exclusively by his dramatic works, this no doubt would be the impression most likely to remain with any thoughtful listener who had not as yet had access to other works showing a very different aspect of his character and genius. But the fact is that d'Indy, for all his alleged Germanic sympathies and admiration for German music, was at the same time a typical Frenchman, with his love of order and precision, and his deep-rooted attachment to the French countryside. At the same time he felt strongly that French music was falling into a rut and was in need of renovation; and all his works are directed towards that end. We need look no further for the explanation of that pronounced kind of spiritual and artistic dichotomy we find, not only in d'Indy's music, but in his general aesthetic and intellectual outlook. On the one hand there was the intellectual aristocrat, inclined to be pedantic and academic, and on the other the forward-looking artist who wanted to be free and independent and above all to advance the cause of music everywhere, not only French music, in accordance with the high ideals which were an essential part of his upbringing.

It seems clear then that the contradictions in his personality and in the expression of his opinions were really due to a conflict within him, between reason and feeling. An example of this can be seen in his attitude towards the music of Debussy, with whom he was on terms of personal friendship but of whose music he did not altogether approve, though he was always ready to conduct it. (Incidentally, this attitude was reciprocated by Debussy who paid generous tribute to d'Indy's lofty ideals while regretting the kind of straitjacket in which their musical expression was too often confined.) A story in this connection well illustrates the way in which d'Indy formed his critical opinions. It is told by M. D. Calvocoressi,[1] who, in conversation with the composer one day, discussing Debussy's *Pelléas et Mélisande*, remarked that what d'Indy was saying at that moment did not seem to tally altogether with what he had written in a recent article. This d'Indy explained by saying that the first time he heard *Pelléas* he listened to it as music, in the

[1] *Musicians' Gallery*, London 1933.

Gabriel Fauré, 1845–1924

Vincent d'Indy, 1851–1931

ordinary sense of the word, as he conceived it, but then, on thinking the matter over again, decided he had been wrong and ought to have listened to it as something altogether different and new. 'So then', he concluded, 'I went to hear it again, and in that new light I was able to admire it.'

The fact that it has always been difficult to arrive at a definite assessment of d'Indy's place in the hierarchy of French musicians of the twentieth century can thus be seen to be due to this dichotomy in his make-up to which I have referred; on the one hand the faithful disciple of César Franck and admirer of the great German musical tradition, and on the other the French aristocrat and patriot whose best works and those by which he is most likely to be remembered were directly inspired by the traditional music and 'ambiance' of that part of the country in which he was born and did most of his actual composing during the summer months. There was also d'Indy the pedagogue and theoretician and author of a remarkable *Cours de composition musicale* in four volumes, and the stern, academic d'Indy of the string quartets and the ponderous Piano Sonata in E major. But of all his varied output the works that have best stood the test of time are those that reflect his love of the countryside where he was born; and so the best of d'Indy, and the most rewarding to a modern listener, is still to be found in such candid and immediately appealing works as (in addition to the *Symphonie Cévenole* already mentioned) the *Poème des montagnes* for piano, the orchestral *Jour d'été à la montagne* and the various collections of *Chansons populaires* from the Cévennes and the Vivarais district where he was born and bred.

He fought as an officer in the Franco-Prussian war, and during the war of 1914–18 he composed a *Sinfonia brevis* (*de bello Gallico*) inspired by these tragic events which did not, however, add greatly to his reputation. Towards the end of his life his music became still more 'French' (he wrote some Mediterranean music during holidays spent on the Côte d'Azur), and as a result of the war his political views were

4*

coloured by even stronger nationalist sentiments, reinforced
by his innate conservatism and fervent Roman Catholic faith.

It is probable that if his works were better known the
stature of d'Indy as a key figure in the evolution of French
music after 1900 would receive the recognition it deserves.
Romain Rolland[1] has paid him the tribute he deserves by
hailing him as 'the chief French representative of the modern
musical renaissance in Europe and, by his action, his example,
his intelligence, as the most powerful educative force in
France'. And with that judgment we can feel that justice has
been done to the memory of Vincent d'Indy, one of the great
musicians of France.

When d'Indy died in 1931, outliving Fauré by seven years,
he had also, in a sense, outlived his epoch. For the musical
scene in France since 1900 had already been radically transformed by the advent of Debussy and Ravel, and also by the
emergence, after the 1914 war, of still another generation of
younger composers who began by planting the flag of revolution, denouncing their immediate predecessors and dreaming
of a new music with no frills, which would be hard and down-
to-earth. The famous group of Six had made their entry.

We shall be examining their achievements in due course, but
three, at least, of their predecessors, all enormously important
figures in twentieth-century French music—Roussel, Koechlin
and Dukas—claim our attention first.

[1] In *Musiciens d'aujourd'hui*.

CHAPTER FOUR

Roussel, Koechlin and Dukas

Albert Roussel (1869–1937) was born in Tourcoing, an industrial town in French Flanders, where his father was a partner in an important firm specialising in carpets and tapestries. He was an only child, and when at the age of eight he had lost both his parents he was placed in the care of his paternal grandfather who was Mayor of Tourcoing, and consequently a very busy man who had little time to devote to the boy, although he supervised his education as best he could and sent him to the local school. When his grandfather died, he went to live with his maternal aunt and her husband who were the first to notice and encourage the boy's interest in music— an interest he had inherited from his mother who had taught him to play the piano and some rudimentary theory—and arranged for him to have further lessons from the local organist.

There was no question, however, of his taking up music as a profession, and at the age of fifteen he had already opted for a career in the Navy. Holidays on the nearby Flanders coast had given him a love for the sea, which was reinforced by his fondness for the tales of Jules Verne, his favourite author. To prepare for entrance into the Ecole Navale the young Roussel was accordingly sent as a boarder to the College Stanislas in Paris; and after passing his Baccalaureat and doing well in the entrance examination for the Navy he joined a training ship at Brest. After serving seven years in the Navy (during which he not only went on several cruises, including one which took him to Cochin-China and other places in the Far East, but also found time to study and even write some music) he took the decision that was to change his whole life and also, as it turned out, the face of French music in the years to come. This momentous step was taken when sub-lieutenant Albert Roussel, at the age of twenty-five, sat down to write his letter of resignation from the Navy in order to devote himself entirely to composition. Thus, like Rimsky-Korsakov, he came to music from the sea. Incidentally, in France there would seem to be a definite connexion between a seafaring life and one or other of the arts, for the novelists Pierre Loti and Claude Farrère were both sailors, while another French composer, who was Roussel's contemporary, Jean Cras, was a sailor all his life, even becoming a Rear-Admiral, and wrote a good deal of his music on the quarter-deck. The circumstance is not without its bearing on the evolution of Roussel the musician, for it was the Navy that gave him the love of travel and the exotic which remained with him all his life, and that passion for the sea (which he shared with Debussy who was a sailor *manqué*) which impelled him to choose as his country retreat, at Varengeville on the Normandy coast, the quiet house whose windows looked out across the English Channel. In the words of a French critic: 'He kept the adventurous spirit of the sailor, and for him each new work was a fresh port of call.'

Roussel was a contemporary of both Debussy and Ravel (the former's junior by seven years and the latter's senior by six), but stylistically he had as little in common with the one as with the other. How he rose to become one of the most important composers of his generation, perfecting a highly individual style of his own after so late a start in his profession, is one of the most remarkable examples of a late-developing genius in musical history. For a brief outline of his career and an objective account of the different phases in his development we need look no further than to a biographical note Roussel himself wrote only four years before his death.[1]

After giving the facts of his early life and career in the navy,

[1] Quoted, by permission of his widow, by Marc Pincherle in his article on the composer in *Histoire de la Musique*, vol. II, *Encyclopédie de la Pléiade*, Paris 1963.

Roussel relates how he studied harmony, counterpoint and fugue with the famous organist Eugène Gigout, and the history of music and orchestration with Vincent d'Indy at the *Schola Cantorum*, where he himself became professor of counterpoint from 1902 to 1914. His musical career, Roussel continues, 'may be divided into three periods. The first, from 1898 to 1913, shows him, after having already produced a few works showing a definite personality, as coming somewhat under the influence of Debussy, although mainly concerned with the solid architectural principles of construction taught by d'Indy. The Trio in E flat, the *Divertissement* for wind and piano, the first four songs, all free from any external influences, foreshadow the definitive works of the third period. On the other hand, the First Symphony, known as *Le Poème de la forêt*, the *Evocations*, a triptych for soloists, chorus and orchestra written after a journey to India, the ballet *Le Festin de l'araignée*, produced in 1913 and which made the composer's reputation, all owe something to the so-called Impressionist school. The production of *Padmâvatî* (1918), an opera-ballet in two acts on a scenario by Louis Laloy, marked the beginning of a transition period to which belong also the symphonic poem *Pour une fête de printemps* and the Second Symphony in B flat. The style is transformed, the harmonic progressions become bolder and more dissonant, the influence of Debussy has completely disappeared, and the new direction taken by the musician where he seems to be exploring new paths, arouses both violent antagonism and enthusiastic approval. Finally, in his third period, the composer seems to have found his final and definitive methods of expression which are universally approved. To the period (1926) belong the Suite in F, the Concerto for small orchestra, the *Psalm 80* for tenor solo, chorus and orchestra, and the Third Symphony in G minor commissioned by the conductor Koussevitsky to celebrate the fiftieth anniversary of the Boston Symphony Orchestra, and which proved to be without doubt one of the most successful of modern symphonies.'

When Roussel drew up this list of his works, one of the most important had not yet been written or produced; this was the ballet with choruses, *Aeneas* (1935), which contains some of his finest music. He might, however, have included his other ballet, *Bacchus et Ariane* (1930), and the *opéra-bouffe* (his only excursion into light music), *Le Testament de la tante Caroline* which was composed in 1933, though not produced at the Opéra-Comique in Paris until the year of his death.

It also seems strange that he did not mention his one-act opera *La Naissance de la lyre* which followed *Padmâvatî* at the Opéra in 1925. Here Roussel turned from the Orient to ancient Greece, and took as his subject the legend of the origin of Apollo's lyre. His librettist was the celebrated Hellenic scholar Théodore Reinach, a personal friend of the composer; the production of this work at the Paris Opéra seemed particularly appropriate, since Garnier's masterpiece is surmounted by the effigy of Apollo holding in his outstretched arms his triumphant lyre.

It is not only today that Roussel's music tends to be underrated and misjudged; he has always been a connoisseur's composer, and even in his lifetime and in his own country it was only a comparatively small minority of critics and practising musicians who saw from the first that here was a new voice speaking with authority and with something new to say. Certainly Roussel himself did nothing to court popularity or make any concessions to the taste of the day. Indeed, he did not believe that music, as he conceived it, should, or even could be popular; for him it was 'the most hermetic and least accessible of all the arts'; and it was this conviction that led him to declare that 'the musician, even more than the poet, is completely isolated in the world, alone with his more or less incomprehensible language'. There might, he conceded, be one or two fine works written expressly for the people . . . 'all the rest, taking into account the relations existing at present between music and the masses, must be destined for the ears of only a very small number'.

This aristocratic attitude is the key to both the man and his music. It was perhaps the only trait he had in common with Debussy, who, despite his humble birth, was the complete intellectual aristocrat, and used to assert that 'art was absolutely useless to the populace'. He even suggested (in a letter to his friend Ernest Chausson) that it might be a good thing to found a 'Society of Musical Esotericism'. Roussel might well have subscribed to this, and would certainly have understood what Montaigne had in mind when he cited the example of the artist, who, on being asked why he laboured so hard at an art which could only be understood by very few, replied: 'J'en ay assez de peu, j'en ay assez d'un, j'en ay assez de pas un.' (I should be content with a few; I should be content with one; I should be content with none at all.)

Roussel from the first made it clear that 'musique pure' was his ideal; 'what I would like to achieve is music that is self-contained ("se satisfaisant à elle-même"); music determined to free itself from any suggestion of the picturesque, completely non-descriptive and unassociated with any particular locality in space. . . . Far from wanting to *describe* anything, I always endeavour to put out of my mind the thought of any objects or forms that might lend themselves to musical description. All I want is to make music.' And at the end of his life Roussel reasserted in still more precise terms his musical *credo*: 'I have always been concerned with design, construction and rhythm and have constantly pursued my researches into questions of form and development.'

There is no doubt that his music would have a much wider appeal had he concerned himself a little more with the purely sensuous quality of its actual sound; but his fondness for somewhat acidulous harmonies and rather dense textures (and this is especially apparent in his writings for the piano) is a sign that his approach to music was intellectual, and that he had very little of the hedonism and delight in beauty of sound for its own sake that distinguishes the music of Debussy. It has

always been difficult to 'situate' Roussel in relation to his
contemporaries, and, indeed, to assess the importance of his
contribution to twentieth-century music in general. Up to now
the tendency has been to underrate him, largely, no doubt, on
account of the relative inaccessibility of much of his music due
to the somewhat hermetic idiom in which it is couched. Yet
the distinction of his mind, the originality of the language he
forged for himself, his rigorous artistic integrity and the sheer
pur sang quality of his musical thought, so evident in all his
major works, certainly entitle him to be considered, along with
Debussy and Ravel, as one of the founders of the 'modern'
movement in music. The respects in which he differed from
Debussy were aptly and epigrammatically expressed by the
French musicologist Paul Landormy, when he said that
'Roussel est quelque chose comme un Debussy formé à l'école
du contrepoint.'

This is a recognition of the fact that Roussel's whole
approach to music was different from Debussy's in so far as it
tended to attach far greater importance to the bones, so to
speak, than to the flesh of whatever musical material he was
handling; and it is this that gives to his music a kind of steely
glitter that one does not find in Debussy. Whereas, with the
latter every musical idea is enveloped in a kind of sensuous
aura, in Roussel's music it is the notes themselves, the inter-
play of moving parts, the logical sequence of ideas and the
rhythmic pulse that, together with the characteristic harmonic
seasoning, are all-important and give to each of his works their
unmistakable and uncompromising individuality. He undoubtedly owed much to his early training under d'Indy at the
Schola Cantorum, and at one time came temporarily but inevitably under the spell of Debussy; but he soon shook off both
these influences, such as they were, and turned away from both
scholastic and Impressionist techniques and ideals to forge for
himself a highly individual style and language of his own. In
this field, indeed, the freeing of the musical vocabulary of his
day from nineteenth-century accretions and harmonic clichés,

Roussel was as much a pioneer in his own very personal way as Debussy and Ravel were in theirs.

It was only natural that some of the peculiarities of his highly individual style were regarded in certain academic circles as evidence of his 'amateurishness' and lack of professional training. It was often said, for example, that his music suffered from having no proper bass line—in the text-book sense of the term; or even that such basses as there were were 'wrong'. A distinguished musician, who knew Roussel well and was himself at one time Director of the Paris Conservatoire, the late Claude Delvincourt, in analysing Roussel's harmonic language[1] has no difficulty in disposing of this accusation (which, as he points out, would be more applicable to Berlioz) and attributes whatever may be idiosyncratic in Roussel's treatment of his bass line to the polytonality which is an essential feature of his style and the basis of all his harmonic thinking. This element of polytonality, or rather bitonality (for his writing is more often bitonal than polytonal), that runs through all his music had already been exploited by some of his younger contemporaries, such as Darius Milhaud and Georges Auric, who were members of the so-called group of 'Les Six', but in a much cruder form. For whereas with them (at least in their early works) the object was primarily to shock for the sake of shocking, with Roussel the procedure was natural to his way of thinking, and invariably used to create an impression of tension or to heighten the poignancy of some emotional situation. Moreover, he always used it with discretion, and his tonal ambiguities, while characteristic of his harmonic style, are never intended to destroy altogether, but rather to enhance the listener's awareness of a basic tonal centre. A good example of what we might call the 'emotional' use of polytonality is to be found in the slow movement of the Third Symphony in G minor (1930) where the use of this device adds a peculiarly poignant flavour to the music. Another work in which this procedure is most effectively employed,

[1] See *La Revue Musicale*, November 1937.

more in this instance for atmospheric than for emotional reasons, is the beautiful but rarely heard symphonic sketch *Pour une fête de Printemps* (1920) which opens with an arrestingly astringent chord consisting of a combination of the triads of D sharp major (or, enharmonically, E flat major) and A major, the effect of which, before it is resolved a few bars later in a perfectly logical fashion, is rather like that of an extra dry Martini on the palate arousing expectancies which are more than fulfilled as the work proceeds.

The importance of Roussel as a symphonist, while not to be exaggerated, tends rather to be overlooked. After all, he had the distinction of being the only French composer of note (with the exception of Alberic Magnard) to have written four symphonies—five, if we count the early *Le Poème de la forêt* (1906) sometimes referred to as his first. Symphonic form has never been particularly congenial to the French musical tem- perament, and until Roussel, very few composers in France had written straightforward, 'classical' symphonies—notably, César Franck, Alberic Magnard, Saint-Saëns, Vincent d'Indy and Paul Dukas—not forgetting Bizet's youthful effort earlier in the nineteenth century. All these symphonies, moreover, had more or less conformed to Germanic tradition, and it was left to Roussel to imprint a definitely Gallic stamp on a form which, since Beethoven, had always been more intensively cultivated in Germany than elsewhere.

Mr. Basil Deane in his interesting study of the composer[1] sees a parallel between Roussel and Schumann in so far as their symphonies are concerned, and calls attention to two main characteristics which these composers had in common: a tem- peramental dualism and the fact that neither was, by the nature of their respective gifts, a born symphonist; for both, as Mr. Deane points out, 'tended to think musically in self-contained ideas which were not susceptible of extended development'. Nevertheless, both composers wrote memorable symphonies, and if neither have had a lasting influence on the evolution of

[1] *Albert Roussel*, Barrie & Rockcliff, London 1961.

symphonic form, this may well be due to the fact that their music was at once too traditional and too personal to provide a model for their successors. The symphonies of Roussel, however, especially the Third and Fourth, are important landmarks in French twentieth-century music and deserve to be better known in this country. So do his other orchestral works, notably the Suite in F (1926) commissioned by Koussevitsky for the fiftieth anniversary of the Boston Symphony Orchestra, the Concerto for small orchestra (1927) and the remarkable symphonic sketch, already mentioned, *Pour une fête de Printemps*. Another outstandingly original work is the Piano Concerto (1927), all too rarely performed, largely, perhaps, because it offers little scope for purely virtuoso pianistic display but calls, on the other hand, for deep musical understanding. Of the big stage works the opera-ballet on an Indian legend, *Padmâvatî* (1918), and the ballets *Aeneas* (1935) and *Bacchus et Ariane* (1930) which contain some of his finest music, are outstanding; while his setting for chorus and orchestra of *Psalm 80* (1928), using the English text, is a fine example of Roussel's ability to combine choral and orchestral forces impressively on a large-scale canvas. Mention should also be made of the symphonic poem for solo voices, chorus and orchestra entitled *Evocations* (1911) and inspired, like *Padmâvatî*, by the composer's attachment to the landscapes and legends of India, in which, as in *Padmâvatî*, he makes use of Hindu scales and rhythms. The early insect-ballet, *Le Festin de l'araignée* (1913), which first brought Roussel's name into prominence just before the first world war, illustrates his ability to enter imaginatively into dramatic situations even in the sub-human world of insect life, and with only small instrumental forces at his disposal, to invest the tragedy of the Spider's Banquet with an aura of uncanny realism and horror.

There are few departments of music to which Roussel did not contribute something of lasting value, and among his works for small instrumental groups the amateur of chamber-music will find much that is rewarding, notably a string quartet

(1932), two violin sonatas (1908 and 1924) and a Serenade for flute, violin, viola, cello and harp (1925). He wrote sympathetically for wind instruments, his last work (unfinished) being in fact a Trio for oboe, clarinet and bassoon on which he was working at the time of his death; while one of the best known of all his chamber works is the four-movement suite for flute and piano entitled *Joueurs de flûte* (1924) the four famous flautists depicted being Pan, Virgil's Tityrus, Krishna and a character from a novel by Henri de Régnier.

Finally, as a song-writer, Roussel will be remembered for some finely chiselled and subtly elusive settings of contemporary French verse and translations from the Chinese; of the latter *La réponse d'une épouse sage* is one of the best known. Not conspicuous for their purely melodic interest (Roussel was not a melodist) and totally devoid of sentimentality, these songs demand from the singer a fine sense of style and an ability to convey every shade of irony, humour, melancholy, levity or tenderness, however discreetly suggested; this is music in which nothing is underlined and from which all emphasis is barred. Among the best-known songs are *Le bachelier de Salamanque*, *Le jardin mouillé*, *Jazz dans la nuit*, *Cœur en péril* and *Sarabande*.

The time has probably not yet come for a final assessment of Roussel's place in European music. It is possible to see in his work here and there perhaps an excessive preoccupation with 'pattern-making', harmonic innovations for their own sake and experiments in construction and design, and to some, his music may seem to be lacking in fire and warmth and human emotions. Yet this music, although completely unsensational, is never frigid. The art of Roussel is characteristically French in its avoidance of sensationalism and over-emphasis; the balance between sentiment and intellect is perfectly preserved and, to sum up, we feel it to be the product of a fine and fastidious mind, nurtured in the best traditions of the humanism that is the basis of our Western civilisation. In paying a last tribute to Roussel, Charles Koechlin, who had been his friend and colleague, found words that could not be bettered and might well serve as his epitaph: 'C'était un artiste complet—un musicien, un penseur, un homme.'

Roussel lived a quiet, retiring life, took no part in musical polemics, but was a shrewd observer of the contemporary scene and always ready to befriend and encourage young composers. His interest in all the latest and most advanced tendencies in music during his lifetime is shown by the fact that he was for a time President of the French section of the International Society for Contemporary Music (I.S.C.M.). His happiest hours were spent in his house by the sea in the company of his wife, and it was there that he composed most of the works by which he will be remembered.

A feature of French music at its highest level has always been its predominantly intellectual character, and French composers have tended to be generally more interested in literature and the other arts and, above all, to be more articulate than those of other nations and more in touch with current cultural trends. This is especially true of musicians of the type of Roussel and his contemporaries in the first decades of this century, and applies not only to Debussy and Ravel, but to men like Charles Koechlin and Paul Dukas, both of whom were not only practising musicians but writers and thinkers as well, of a wide general culture. In fact what all these men and many others besides of their generation believed in firmly as a kind of artistic Credo, was perfectly expressed by Roussel when he paid that tribute (see p. 9) to the elevating influence of the arts, and of music in particular, seeing in them the only foundation on which a truly civilised society can be built. There can have been few periods in musical history where the truth of this doctrine and awareness of it had been so clearly manifested as during these years in France which witnessed a spectacular flowering of musical talents almost without precedent, when one considers its rare quality and the fact that it was all concentrated within so short a space of time, something less than half a century. For the centre of musical gravity was now unquestionably in France, and Teutonic supremacy, potent though it had been in its time, now a thing of the past. Roussel's conception of a civilised society was now very much a reality, and music as one of its most essential ingredients was safe in the hands of a band of exceptionally gifted and dedicated artists.

Of these, one of the most remarkable, but still insufficiently known, was Roussel's contemporary Charles Koechlin (1867–1950) who occupies a very special place in this particular period of French musical history. He came of an Alsatian family of industrialists established at Mulhouse, and was brought up in an atmosphere of Protestant liberalism which coloured his whole attitude towards life and art. Like Roussel, Koechlin came to music late at the age of twenty-two, after graduating from the Ecole Polytechnique in Paris. At the Conservatoire he came under the influence of Fauré, but though he developed slowly, even his earliest compositions already showed marked originality. He never adhered to any particular school or system, but there was hardly any branch of music to which he did not make some important contribution, and hardly any style or idiom with which he did not experiment at one time or another—polytonality, atonality, strict contrapuntal polyphony, even strict twelve-note serialism; while some of his best and most characteristic work is couched in the simplest diatonic or modal language.

He was a prolific composer, and his works (many of which are still unpublished, but the MSS. are now deposited in the Bibliothèque Nationale) cover an immense field from songs, pianoforte music and every variety of chamber combination to large-scale orchestral and choral works, lyric drama, ballets, film-music and last, but not least, an important corpus of pedagogic and theoretical works including a *Treatise on Harmony* in three volumes. He also wrote copiously on musical topics in the musical press, and was the author of biographies of Debussy and Fauré.

Everything he wrote reflects an original mind and a breadth

of outlook and grasp of every conceivable aspect of musical theory and practice that has few parallels in the annals of music. Yet he remained to the last uninfluenced by any particular school or fashionable '-ism' current in his lifetime, while feeling free to express himself in any idiom which seemed to him best suited to whatever work he had in hand. Despite this stylistic eclecticism, all his music bears the stamp of a very individual and highly original musical personality. Independence, breadth of outlook and complete intellectual and moral integrity were Koechlin's outstanding qualities, and these were combined with an almost child-like candour and simplicity which give to much of his music its uniquely appealing quality. The *Sonatines* for piano notably reflect this side of his genial nature as do many of his songs and simpler instrumental works.

Koechlin, for all his immense erudition and familiarity with music of all ages, was far from being a pedant. On the contrary he took a keen interest in the contemporary scene, and was alive to every trend and every new development in the music of his time. In the nineteen-thirties he became interested in the world of the cinema, and besides composing some film scores himself (which never, however, reached the screen) he wrote a symphonic suite in seven movements (The 'Seven Stars' Symphony) each of which is dedicated to the seven most famous film stars in America at that time (1933): Douglas Fairbanks, Lilian Harvey, Greta Garbo, Clara Bow, Marlene Dietrich, Emil Jannings and Charlie Chaplin. He also wrote a set of *Danses pour Ginger* (1937) 'en hommage à Ginger Rogers'. The catholicity of his tastes and wide reading is shown by the authors whose works he either set or derived inspiration from; these include Romain Rolland and André Gide (scenes from *Jean-Christophe* and a *Hymne à la jeunesse* inspired by a chapter from *Voyage d'Urien*); Heinrich Heine (symphonic poem *En mer la nuit* based on Heine's *North Sea*); H. G. Wells (symphonic poem *La cité nouvelle, rêve d'avenir*, dedicated to the writer); Pierre Loti (*Les heures Persanes* for piano); and numerous settings of Leconte de Lisle, Verlaine, Pierre Louÿs, Tristan Klingsor (poems from *Shéhérazade*, but not the same as those set by Ravel) and Paul Claudel.

But it was Rudyard Kipling's *The Jungle Book* that inspired Koechlin to write the music by which he is most likely to be remembered, beginning with the *Trois poèmes du Livre de la Jungle* (composed between 1899 and 1910: *The seal's lullaby*, *Chanson de la nuit dans la jungle* and *Chant de Kala Nag*) for chorus and orchestra, followed by the four symphonic poems *La Course de Printemps* (Spring Running) (1925-7), *Méditation de Prun Baghat* (1936), *La loi de la Jungle* (1939) and *Les Bandar-Log* (1939-40).[1] These works, especially the last-named, together with the very remarkable Second Symphony (1943-4) reveal Koechlin as a master of the first order, high-lighting his expert handling of large orchestral forces, the boldness of his harmonic language, grasp of form and the startling originality of his musical ideas and methods of expressing them.

From first to last during his long career Koechlin was a pioneer. Already in some of his earliest works, notably in *La fin de l'homme* (Leconte de Lisle) (1895) and *L'Abbaye* (1899-1902), both for solo voices, chorus and orchestra, he was using harmonic procedures which at the time were most unusual; for example, the mingling of triads containing augmented fifths and the construction of chords composed of fourths and fifths superimposed which was one of his most characteristic harmonic devices to be met with frequently in his later works, e.g., the two books of *Paysages et marines* for piano. He was also, a fact that is not perhaps generally known, one of the first to practise polytonality which he looked upon as a natural extension of the scales associated with the modal music of the middle ages into which he was initiated while still a student by Bourgault-Ducoudray (1840-1910) who was then Professor of musical history at the Paris Conservatoire. It was in this way, as the Belgian musicologist Paul Collaer has pointed out in his book on *Modern Music*, that Koechlin, 'thanks to the diversity

[1] Recorded in *Music Today* series EMI ALP 2092/ASD639.

Albert Roussel, 1869–1950

Paul Valéry, 1871–1945

of modal music inherited from both Gregorian chant and French folk-song, escaped from what Maurice Emmanuel denounced as 'the tyranny of the major-minor scale', and passed over from simple tonality to polytonality . . . he was the first to develop the possibilities of this kind of counterpoint and harmony, preparing the way for Darius Milhaud. . . .' The latter and his fellow-members of the 'Group of Six' are usually credited with being pioneers in this field; but it is clear that it was the example of Koechlin that inspired them. Indeed, long before Milhaud had started to compose, Koechlin had written his viola sonata (1913–15), which he described as 'uninhibitedly bitonal' and of which Milhaud, to whom it is dedicated, gave the first performance. In his later works Koechlin did not hesitate to introduce atonal passages when it suited his purpose to do so (but never for effect or to suggest his adherence to this or to any other 'system'); and one of the most effective examples of his use of atonality is to be found in the *Bandar-Log* when he ironically makes the monkeys, who are supposed to be showing off their up-to-date-ness and modernity, express themselves in this language. Henri Sauguet, who was his pupil and is one of his most ardent admirers, has admirably summed up all the great qualities and gifts that seem to put Koechlin in a class apart, so that (to quote his words) 'his personality dominates our contemporary musical universe', in the following eloquent tribute: 'To obey only his own laws, to make concessions to no one but himself, to heighten his means of expression to match the noblest as well as the most subtle flights of his thought, to speak all languages whenever this seems necessary regardless of formulae, schools, dogmas or cliques, to allow himself to be guided by his instinct alone—or rather by his genius as an artist—these are the qualities which are the very essence of the whole art of Charles Koechlin. Add to all this a deep sympathy with Nature in all its aspects with which he had been all his life in close communion, a compulsive attraction to the world of dreams and that intimate participation in the eternal life of the universe which is the privilege

5—M.F.M.

of great men, and there you have the magic Jungle from which
the art and personality of Charles Koechlin emerges as one of
the most curious, the most surprising, the richest, the most
mysterious and the most dominating of our time.'[1]

This is high praise, but is typical of the veneration with
which Koechlin was regarded by all who came in contact with
him, from the youngest of his pupils to the most eminent
among his contemporaries—and these included men like
Duparc, Fauré, Roussel, Debussy, Ravel and countless others;
for it must not be forgotten that not only did he have a powerful, formative influence on the young composers who came to
him for guidance, but was at the same time admired and respected by his contemporaries. Thus he enjoyed the confidence
of both Fauré and Debussy, who entrusted him with the
orchestration of important works—notably the incidental
music that Fauré wrote for the London production of Maeterlinck's play *Pelléas et Mélisande* in 1898, and the music composed
by Debussy for the English dancer Maud Allan's ballet
Khamma. And, as one discerning French critic has pointed out,
both these orchestrations 'reveal a profound understanding of
the ultra-refined technique of these two masters. In *Khamma*
especially, where the orchestration is of prime importance,
Charles Koechlin has displayed the full extent of his intelligent
virtuosity.'

In the course of his long life Koechlin witnessed the unfold-
ing of a whole new era in Western music, from the first nights
of *Pelléas et Mélisande* in 1902 and of Stravinsky's *Rite of Spring*
in 1913 to the revelation of Anton Webern whose music did
not reach France until after the Liberation. And during that
time he had been a co-founder, with Ravel, André Caplet and
Florent Schmitt, of the Société Musicale Indépendante; had
been the friend and admirer of Erik Satie; had witnessed the
formation of the group of 'Les Six' and the 'Ecole d'Arcueil'
(disciples of Satie) and other progressive groups such as the

[1] Henri Sauguet: 'Charles Koechlin poète de la Jungle', *Arts*, 1 January
1953.

Triton and *Jeune France*, and (always a keen supporter of the 'new' music) had found time to be Président d'Honneur of the French section of the International Society for Contemporary Music (I.S.C.M.) whose festivals he regularly attended till the end of his life. And there must be many readers who recall his noble, patriarchal appearance, with his long white beard and black flowing cloak, and that simplicity of bearing and courtesy towards all and sundry which was the hallmark of the great man and great artist that was Charles Koechlin, a key figure in the evolution of French music in the twentieth century.

An almost exact contemporary of both Koechlin and Roussel, and a musician of comparable intellectual and artistic calibre, was Paul Dukas (1865–1935) who had been as a boy in the same composition class at the Paris Conservatoire as Debussy, and during his lifetime had been a shrewd observer of, as well as a participant in, the exciting developments in French music that had marked the end of the nineteenth and beginning of the twentieth century. Dukas was a scholarly type of musician and a perfectionist, and consequently though a fastidious artist he was not a prolific composer, although everything he wrote is marked by a high degree of craftsmanship as well as of poetic and imaginative inspiration. The word 'poetic' is appropriate, because he himself used to say that, in the last resort, all art is poetry; and it was just that quality in his music—that element of 'poésie pure'—that his great friend, the poet Paul Valéry, especially admired.

Known to most music-lovers as the composer of *L'Apprenti sorcier*, the work that brought him fame overnight after he had conducted it himself at a Société Nationale concert in Paris in 1897, Dukas has never received outside France—and not always within it—the recognition due to him as the creator of at least two other outstanding works—the opera *Ariane et Barbe-Bleue* and the Variations, for piano, on a theme of Rameau, not to mention other important works such as the Symphony in C and a monumental Piano Sonata in E flat minor of which

Alfred Cortot has said that it 'represents one of the most important efforts ever made to adapt Beethovenian characteristics to the French pianistic style'. Cortot also declares that this Sonata, which he describes as 'this magnificent edifice in sound', 'has its place in the front rank of the lasting monuments consecrated by the French school to the glory of the piano'.

Dukas' other outstanding contribution to the literature of the piano, the *Variations, Interlude et Finale sur un thème de Rameau* is, like the Sonata, conceived on a grand scale, and confronts the performer with formidable technical and intellectual problems which perhaps accounts for the fact that so few pianists today seem prepared to tackle it. This is another work of truly Beethovenian proportions and, indeed, can fairly be compared in some ways to the Diabelli Variations of Beethoven, at least in so far as, while the theme itself is trivial, the treatment it is subjected to, making, as it were, a mountain out of a molehill, is both ingenious and elaborate, and a challenge to any pianist's powers of execution and interpretation.

The immediate success and world-wide renown of *L'Apprenti sorcier*, which first brought the name of Dukas before the general public, was well deserved; for this dazzling picture in sound of the tribulations that befell the disobedient sorcerer's apprentice in Goethe's ballad is a little masterpiece of 'representational' music, most imaginatively conceived and brilliantly carried out. The composer's mastery of the orchestra and command of every refinement of instrumental colour is already apparent; and it is these same qualities, raised to an even higher level that give a rare distinction to the opera *Ariane et Barbe-Bleue* which was perhaps Dukas' most important contribution to the music of our time. In the libretto, written specially for Dukas by Maeterlinck (whose *Pelléas et Mélisande* had already been set by Debussy), a new variant of the well-known Blue-Beard legend is proposed whereby Ariane persuades Blue-Beard to allow her to offer the other captive wives their freedom. And when they are too timid to accept it, preferring the captivity they know to a liberty of which they are afraid, Blue-Beard does nothing to prevent Ariane herself from leaving the Castle and returning to the light of day.

The opera contains some memorable scenes, the poignancy and pathos of which are enhanced by the eloquent music, rich in colour and marked by a rare degree of lyrical intensity and dramatic feeling. It was performed for the first time at the Paris Opéra-Comique in May 1907, just five years after the first performance at the same theatre of Debussy's *Pelléas*, a work which Dukas had always admired, and to which, perhaps inevitably, his own opera owed something indirectly, if only in its awareness of the new musical language for which the innovations of Debussy had prepared the way. And after Debussy's death in 1918 Dukas paid a moving homage to his memory in the form of a short piece for the piano entitled *La plainte au loin du Faune*, which was almost his last published work. His last major work was, in fact, the 'Poème dansé' *La Péri* written for Diaghilev, and danced by Nijinsky and Trouhanova in 1912—a most memorable contribution to the repertoire of Ballet in which once again, as in the opera *Ariane*, Dukas exhibits his mastery of the orchestra and command of every refinement of instrumental colour.

Despite the fact that he lived to the age of seventy, the number of his published works is remarkably small. For the last twenty-three years of his life he published practically nothing, though this does not mean that he gave up composing altogether. Being highly self-critical, if he thought that any work of his did not wholly satisfy his own exacting standards of perfection, he preferred to destroy it—and in fact, when asked by his friend, the composer Georges Enesco, shortly before he died what he was proposing to do with the manuscripts which were known to exist, he replied: 'Mon cher Georges, j'ai tout brûlé.'

From 1913 to the end of his life Dukas was professor of composition at the Paris Conservatoire and at the *Ecole Normale de musique*, and in 1934 was elected to the Académie des

Beaux Arts in succession to Alfred Bruneau. He was also a writer of great distinction, and contributed articles on music to various important journals, many of which were later collected and published posthumously in book form under the title *Les écrits de Paul Dukas sur la musique*. Wide knowledge, high principles, a keen critical sense and an acute and scholarly mind characterise everything he wrote. Certain aspects of contemporary music, however, disturbed him; and his attitude towards what is sometimes called 'progress' can be summed up in a remark he once made: 'There is no such thing as new music; there are only new musicians.'

Such was Paul Dukas; a somewhat neglected figure in the annals of the music of this period, but one whose importance is undeniable and deserves more generous recognition.

CHAPTER FIVE

BACKGROUND TO DEBUSSY'S FORMATIVE YEARS; SYMBOLISM AND
IMPRESSIONISM IN POETRY, PAINTING AND MUSIC; RIMBAUD AND
THE *Alchimie du Verbe*; MALLARMÉ'S *Faun* AND MAETERLINCK'S
Pelléas RE-BORN IN THE MUSIC OF DEBUSSY

In the panorama of music since 1900 outlined so far we have
been dealing mainly with five distinguished French composers
all of whom, though contemporaries for a time of Debussy,
outlived him by from six to nineteen years having, unlike him,
survived the first world war. And so it is against the background of their solid achievements and individual contributions to the musical renaissance that was taking place in France
that we must now consider the special case of Debussy who,
more than any other of his contemporaries, not excepting
Ravel, is now recognised as the key figure in the movement of
liberation that led to what is now commonly known as
'modern music'.

It was Charles Koechlin who said that 'no artist in the history
of French music had ever arrived more precisely at his
appointed time than Claude Debussy'. By this he meant that
there was a happy coincidence between the current aesthetic
climate and his own particular tastes and natural disposition.
What the epoch had to offer was something with which his
own genius was in sympathy. There was the *fin de siècle* element
with all that that implied; and there was also the forward-
looking trend that accompanied the beginning of a new century. Debussy extracted the best out of both, and reflected in
his music the atmosphere and aspirations of a changing world.
Tristan and *Parsifal* still cast their long shadows everywhere; in
England the rather precious aestheticism of Dante Gabriel
Rossetti and the Pre-Raphaelites was preparing the way for

l'Art Nouveau; while Aubrey Beardsley and Algernon Swinburne with brush and pen were extolling, in a last flicker of
fin-de-siècle decadence, with undercurrents of erotic perversity,
in contrast to the 'lilies and languors of virtue, the raptures
and roses of vice.'

In France, Baudelaire, Verlaine and Mallarmé and the so-
called Symbolists were opening up new areas of sensibility, and
narrowing the borders between poetry and music, while in
painting the Impressionists, with new theories about light and
vision, were looking at Nature with their own eyes instead of
through the distorting spectacles of academic theory.

Caught between these two main currents of Symbolism and
Impressionism, Debussy responded sympathetically to both at
first, though the mistake so often made of labelling his music
'Impressionist' provoked him more than once to disclaiming
the imputation altogether. 'What I am trying to do', he wrote
once to his publisher *à propos* one of his orchestral *Images*, 'is to
create a kind of reality—what these imbeciles call "Impressionism".'

But since these were, in fact, the principal influences to
which Debussy was exposed, at any rate during his adolescence
and early youth, it is necessary to explain as far as possible the
sense in which these terms are commonly used in connexion
with developments in French literature and art at the turn of
the century.

Impressionism is the easier to understand, though the term
is loosely used and cannot in fact be exactly defined. In contrast to 'realism' which aims at portraying the 'thing itself' by
using means that approximate as closely as possible to the subject by which the artist is inspired so that the result will be as
nearly as possible a *transcription* rather than a *translation* of his
actual impressions in whatever medium he may be working
(cf. Mussorgsky, the greatest 'realist' in music), Impressionism
is more likely to be subjective, its object being to reproduce in
paint or sound (or, for that matter, words) the 'impression'
made on the artist, in a purely subjective sense, by whatever he

may be contemplating at any given moment. The difference between the two techniques is like the generic difference between painting and photography: the one, Impressionism, is essentially a reconstruction (subjective), the other an imitation (objective). Nevertheless, paradoxically enough, Impressionism in painting owed its origin to a desire for greater scientific precision, and the first Impressionists were concerned above all to bring their painting into line with certain definite scientific laws relating to light and the refraction of the sun's rays. Monet's studies of the Cathedral of Rouen, for example, seen first in shade and then in sunlight, are definitely impressionistic in their technique; but in a sense they are also realistic—that is to say, they are not a transformation of the subject governed purely by arbitrary laws of abstract harmony (e.g. certain of the *Nocturnes* or *Symphonies* of Whistler) but a representation of a certain aspect of the subject as it actually appeared to the artist.

This 'Impressionistic' style in painting[1] soon, by a natural transition, began to have an influence on music. It only remained to translate the Impressionist theory from terms of light to terms of sound, and for musicians to put it into practice. Blurred outlines were soon found to be just as feasible in music as in painting, and the scintillating effects of sunlight found their counterpart in shimmering harmonies and the skilfully blended vibrations of the harmonic 'upper partials'. Just as the painters 'decomposed' a ray of light, so did the musicians split up the 'fundamental' of a chord into its component parts; and to this extent it would perhaps be true to say that Debussy was the first composer to employ the Impressionist technique.

The term 'Symbolism', on the other hand, was applied more

[1] The term might never have been coined had not Claude Monet once given to one of his pictures exhibited in 1874 the title *Impression: soleil levant*, which caused a Parisian critic immediately to label all the painters exhibiting with Monet on that occasion—Cézanne, Degas, Morisot, Pissarro, Renoir, Sisley, etc.—'Impressionistes'.

specifically to literature, but its exact meaning is more difficult to define. In contrast to the so-called 'Parnassiens', headed by Théophile Gautier (1811–1872), whose ideal was to combine extreme sensibility with a precision of language and a high degree of technical perfection, the Symbolists on the other hand aimed at an extreme fluidity of versification, and believed that it was the function of poetry to suggest, not to describe, and to portray, if anything, the poet's own states of mind and consciousness rather than the external world. Symbolist poetry also aspired to the state of music, relying on the effect produced by its sound quite as much as by its sense. The leading Symbolist poets in France were Stéphane Mallarmé (1841–1898), Charles Baudelaire (1821–1867), Paul Verlaine (1844–1896), Arthur Rimbaud (1854–1891), Henri de Régnier (1864–1936), Jean Moréas (1856–1910) and Jules Laforgue (1860–1887), one of the pioneers of *vers libre*. A typical Symbolist work of fiction is Huysman's famous 'decadent' novel, *A rebours* (1884), while the greatest name in the theatre of Symbolism is Maurice Maeterlinck (1862–1949), whose dramas of mystery and anguish, with their nebulous characters expressing themselves in semi-articulate speech in settings heavily charged with symbolism, were admirably adapted to musical treatment, as Debussy was to discover when he came to turn *Pelléas et Mélisande* into the unique opera with which his name will always be linked, and which remains one of the greatest masterpieces of twentieth-century music.

There have been many attempts to define Symbolism. Baudelaire's quatrain stresses its aesthetic and philosophical basis:

> La nature est un temple où de vivants piliers
> Semblent sortir parfois de confuses paroles;
> L'homme y marche à travers des forêts de symboles
> Qui l'observent avec des regards familiers.

(Nature is a temple where, from living pillars confused speech seems sometimes to emerge; Man walks there amidst a forest of symbols which watch him from familiar eyes.)

The German philosopher Novalis (Friedrich Leopold von Hardenburg, 1772–1801) who dreamed of an ideal synthesis in which art and life and religion would be one, was expressing what symbolism's inner meaning really is when he said that 'everything visible has its roots in the invisible'; and the same idea must have been in the poet Paul Valéry's mind when in a letter to Mallarmé he defined the Symbolists' ideal of an art '. . . unissant le monde qui nous entoure au monde qui nous hante'. 'Uniting the world in which we live with the world which haunts our thoughts'—this surely is a profound and admirable definition of what art in essence is, and not only as it may appear when seen through Symbolist eyes.

But the aspect of Symbolism that concerns us now is the extent to which it influenced musicians, and also poets and writers, in their views about the relation between music and literature. This, in fact, was a burning question which began to agitate the literary world in the last decade of the nineteenth century, and is in itself an interesting phenomenon for, until Wagner began to cast his spell, most literary men in the 'sixties and 'seventies were either uninterested in, or detested music— for example: Victor Hugo, Balzac, the Goncourts, Théophile Gautier (although he wote about it), Lamartine, etc. But then came Baudelaire, Verlaine ('de la musique avant toute chose'), Rimbaud, and especially poets like Mallarmé and Valéry who both wrote 'musical' verse but at the same time were alive to the dangers of too close a union between music and letters. They envied music's power (as late as 1935 Valéry was speaking of 'la puissance de la musique qui se développe tellement') and sought ways of somehow transferring these powers to literature: 'Reprendre à la musique son bien' was Valéry's phrase; but Mallarmé distrusted music's purely sensuous appeal, and conceived it rather as an ideal state existing primarily in the mind. It would seem, in fact, from his various cryptic remarks on the subject, that he approved of music except for the noise it makes, which he thought disturbing to the understanding.[1] Thus it was wrong to suppose that the Pythagorean 'music of the spheres' was perceptible to the ear; rather was it meant to suggest a blend between hearing and a kind of abstract vision which becomes Understanding. Fundamentally, then, what Mallarmé objected to in music was its appeal to the Unconscious mind rather than to the Intellect or Understanding, since for him, ideally, music as its name suggests, meant everything that had to do with the Muses, and nothing to do with instruments or physical sound. With this conception of music as an 'art du silence' in mind he was able to speak of 'un solitaire tacite concert . . .' and to justify a union between music and poetry, but on a footing of equality since, for him, 'la Poésie proche l'Idée, est Musique par excellence, ne consent pas d'infériorité'. On the whole, then, Mallarmé agreed with Kant, who said that from a rational point of view music had less value than any of the other fine arts, rather than with Schopenhauer who maintained that music is the supreme form of Art—an art of Will—and superior to poetry which he called the art of language and superficial reason.

Nevertheless, we have it on the evidence of Paul Valéry that Mallarmé used to attend concerts, and could often be seen at the Cirque d'Eté (where the Concerts Lamoureux used to take place) 'experiencing with delight, but with that angelic suffering that comes from a conflict between superior forces, the magic spell of Beethoven or Wagner. . . . Mallarmé after these concerts was filled with a sublime jealousy. He tried desperately to find a means of regaining for our art the important and marvellous qualities which all too powerful Music was stealing from it.'

[1] The kind of music he was afraid of, in fact, was what Wagner had in mind when he said that, for him, 'music is something demoniacal, a mystical and sublime monstrosity; any kind of *rule* violates its essential nature . . . form is plastic, not musical, based on reason, impoverished reason, while music evolves in sentiments of the sublime . . .'.

All this shows how right Paul Valéry was when he said (in a speech delivered on 4 January 1931 celebrating the fiftieth anniversary of the Lamoureux Concerts in Paris) that 'Any literary history of the late nineteenth century that contains no reference to music would be useless; a history worse than incomplete—inexact; worse than inexact—unintelligible. Every epoch has its main sources of stimulation, and centres of interest, and these are always reflected more or less directly in the literature of the day. And I am convinced that it is impossible to understand anything about the movement in poetry since 1840–50 down to the present day unless the significance of the profoundly important part played by music in this remarkable transformation is stressed, and its nature explained and defined. The musical education of the public in France—and particularly of an increasing number of French writers—has contributed more than any theoretical considerations to ensuring for poetry a purer future, and eliminating from it everything that can be better expressed in prose.

'Just as music, in the beginning, divided aural impressions into two categories, rejecting mere *noises*, which may mean *something* but which cannot easily be combined, but accepting *sounds* which, meaningless by themselves, can yet very well be reproduced and combined, so has poetry endeavoured, sometimes with great difficulty and at great risk, to distinguish (to the best of its ability) in language those expressions in which meaning, rhythm, sound and movement complement and reinforce one another, while excluding those in which the meaning is independent of musical form and sound.

'This re-education, as it were, of poetry (between 1880 and 1900) was largely the result of the Lamoureux Concerts. While Baudelaire had Pasdeloup, Mallarmé and his successors had Lamoureux; . . . and to the youth of that generation the emotion they experienced through hearing great music, and especially orchestral music, gave them a feeling of confidence and strength. . . . Such great music radiates a kind of excessive aesthetic energy. It evokes the depths of life, and extremes of passion; imitates the processes of thought, and seems to stir up Nature. It agitates and soothes, and plays on the whole nervous system—and all these effects are obtained irresistibly and almost instantaneously, sometimes through a single note.... No other art can claim such supremacy; it is not surprising, then, that music like this has become a cult. . . .'[1]

It had, indeed, become so much a cult that at the end of the nineteenth century the poets were already trying to create in their verse purely musical effects, and writers like Mallarmé and Rimbaud were handling words in much the same way as the painters and musicians were treating light and sound. They constructed their sentences on an almost purely musical basis, aiming not only at broad rhythmic effects, but also at the establishment of a regular harmonic system in which vowels and consonants should play the part of notes in a chord, with cadences, resolutions and other refinements borrowed from musical techniques. The Symbolists also aimed at visual effects, and by the skilful isolation of rare and vivid words, scattered here and there like jewels, sought to evoke, by the association of ideas, a host of suggestive images. Rimbaud, indeed, as is well known, went as far as to invest the vowels with colour 'A noir, E blanc, I rouge, O bleu, U vert.' ' Je règlai', he wrote, 'la forme et le mouvement de chaque consonne et, avec des rythmes instinctifs, je me flattai d'inventer un verbe poétique accessible, un jour ou l'autre, à tous les sens.'

Similarly, one of the chief theoreticians of the Symbolist movement, the poet René Ghil in his *Traité du Verbe* (1886) imagined a system of 'verbal instrumentation' in which, for example, each vowel, like each instrument in an orchestra, would have its own *timbre*, thus enabling the poet to 'orchestrate' his poem scientifically. And, indeed, Mallarmé, in one of his most abstruse poems, *Un coup de dés jamais n'abolira le hasard*, in an attempt to put into practice Ghil's theories, did in fact achieve a kind of verbal orchestration by arranging groups of words like notes, using spaces like staves and varying the type

[1] Paul Valéry: *Pièces sur l'Art*, Paris 1934.

to imitate crotchets, quavers, etc. This has inspired another critic, Claude Roulet in his *Eléments de poétique Mallarméenne* (1947) to suggest that the poem was actually a strict fugue, with subject, counter-subject, and stretti, with a Coda and various kinds of canon; he even speaks of 'a modulation prolonged by a miniscule *decrescendo* of pizzicato violins and cellos over a pedal-point . . .'.

The text of this poem is, in any case, one of the curiosities of literature, and from the specimen page reproduced overleaf[1] the reader will be able to form his own opinion as to how far the typographical eccentricities can really be said to approximate to musical notation.

There is no doubt, of course, that this whole movement in French literature in the 'nineties stemmed, at least in part, from the theories of Wagner which had been assiduously propagated in the *Revue Wagnérienne* which was in existence from 1885 until 1888 and numbered among its contributors some of the most distinguished musicians and writers of the day. Among the latter were Mallarmé, Gérard de Nerval, J. K. Huysmans, Verlaine, Catulle Mendès and Villiers de l'Isle Adam; while the musicians included such famous names as Liszt, Saint-Saëns, Vincent d'Indy, Alfred Bruneau, Gabriel Fauré and Florent Schmitt. So far as the Symbolists are concerned, it is clear that they were influenced by Wagner's theories about the 'Gesamtkunstwerk', a fusion of all the arts resulting in a 'total art' in which, notably, the barriers between the spoken word and music would be broken down, each complementing the other, but at the same time jealously on the look-out lest one should dare to poach on the other's preserves. And if at any time it was literature that seemed to be threatened, then the cry was, as we have seen, 'reprendre à la musique son bien—even to the extent of 'orchestrating' words as Mallarmé and his followers were credited with doing.

No study of developments in twentieth-century music would be complete without at least a reference to this question of the

[1] By kind permission of Penguin Books Ltd. from *Mallarmé*, ed. A. Hartley, pp. 226–7.

soucieux

    expiatoire et pubère

        muet

        La lucide et seigneuriale aigrette
          au front invisible
        scintille
          puis ombrage
        une stature mignonne ténébreuse
          en sa torsion de sirène

        par d'impatientes squames ultimes

---

inter-relation between music and letters and the extent to which composers like Debussy and others of his generation were affected by it; and there exists a considerable body of literature on the subject, although it always remained very much a matter for specialists and soon fell out of fashion.[1] After the 1914 war, in fact, there was a strong reaction against the whole idea of a fusion of the arts, and the pendulum of fashion swung emphatically in the opposite direction. Now it was a point of principle among artists to keep their arts distinct and independent of each other; the tendency now was to stress the differences rather than the points of resemblance between

[1] For a well-documented and exhaustive treatment of this whole question see, e.g., Suzanne Bernard: *Mallarmé et la Musique*, Paris 1959, which contains also a full bibliography; also articles in *La Revue Musicale*, Jan. 1952, notably 'Mallarmé et la musique du silence' by Aimé Patri.

> rire
>
>   *que*
>
>   *SI*
>
>   *de vertige*
>
>   *debout*
>
>   *le temps*
>   *de souffleter*
>   *bifurquées*
>
>   *un roc*
>   *faux manoir*
>   *tout de suite*
>   *évaporé en brumes*
>
>   *qui imposa*
>   *une borne à l'infini*

them; and 'pure' music, 'pure' poetry and 'pure' painting
were the new aesthetic slogans. With this went a rejection of
subject or content or, especially in music, expression, and soon
neo-classicism was on its way.

There is, however, another aspect of the new poet-musician
relationship which has to be considered, namely the extent to
which composers were directly influenced by current literary
trends. For, since the actual techniques of music and literature
had now been brought nearer than ever before, it was only
natural that, while the poets were borrowing from music,
musicians on the other hand should have shown themselves to
be especially sensitive to contemporary literature. Two of the
greatest French song-writers, Fauré and Duparc were pioneers
in this field, but it was left to Debussy, whose settings of
Baudelaire, Mallarmé and Verlaine in particular have never

6—M.F.M.

been equalled for their extraordinary sensitiveness to the mood and intentions of the poet, to bring about the final consecration of the union of poetry and music. Leaving aside for the moment the actual songs, which will be considered in the chapter that follows, it would be appropriate in this context to consider for a moment the various literary influences which, at one time or another, were reflected in Debussy's work before taking a longer look at the two major works in which the fusion between the poet's and the musician's inspiration is most complete: the *Prélude à l'après-midi d'un Faune* and *Pelléas et Mélisande*. In parenthesis, when one recalls that Debussy had virtually no education as a child it seems astonishing that he was able, merely by extensive reading and his contact with other artists, to keep abreast with every new movement in the arts, not only in France but in other countries as well. One of the earliest of these influences was that of the Pre-Raphaelites in England, and notably the poetry of D. G. Rossetti which he had come across in a French translation in Gabriel Sarrazin's book *Les poètes modernes de l'Angleterre* while he was still a student in residence at the Villa Medici in Rome. An immediate result of this encounter was the composition of his first important large-scale work, the cantata for orchestra, female chorus and solo voices *La Damoiselle élue*, a setting of Rossetti's *Blessed Damozel* in which already Debussy reveals his extraordinary gift of fitting music to words so intimately that the music becomes, as it were, impregnated with the poetic content, and the poetry born again as music. Unlike Wagner who thought it was music's role to fertilise poetry, Debussy on the contrary believed that poetry should fertilise music; and in this case there is no doubt that, having once come under the spell (if only temporarily) of the Pre-Raphaelites, he promptly produced a perfect and authentic piece of Pre-Raphaelite music. Though today *La Damoiselle élue* may seem to us hardly more than a rather faded period piece, the scoring already shows signs of the mature Debussy and, as a musical counterpart to Rossetti's rather sickly and mannered poem, it is extraordinarily successful. The verdict of the Académie des Beaux Arts, when *La Damoiselle* was submitted to them as an 'envoi de Rome' (works submitted by students awarded the 'Prix de Rome'), was lukewarm. 'The text chosen', so the report ran, 'is rather obscure, but the music is not deficient either in poetry or charm, although it still bears the marks of that systematic tendency towards vagueness of expression and form of which the Academy has already complained. . . .' A typically academic reaction to non-conformism, and evidence already of Debussy's independence and defiance of convention.

Besides the work of the Pre-Raphaelites there is evidence[1] that Debussy was also acquainted with the poetry of Swinburne, some of which, notably the *Poems and Ballads*, had been translated into French by his friend Gabriel Mourey as early as 1891. But the main foreign literary influence, which became for Debussy almost an obsession, was that of the American poet and fantasist Edgar Allan Poe, whose impact on a whole generation of French writers and artists had been most marked thanks mainly to Baudelaire's translations of the 'Tales' (*Histoires extraordinaires*, and *Nouvelles histoires extraordinaires*) which he published as early as 1856/7. Although Poe died in 1849, his influence on French literature lasted well into the 'nineties, and, as Mr. Lockspeiser has pertinently remarked,[2] 'None of the writers in the rich generation from Baudelaire to Paul Valéry, including Gide and Marcel Proust, escaped his fascination; and the aspect of Poe to which they were drawn was the rising to the surface of unconscious fantasies. . . . The Symbolist figures in French literature, from Baudelaire onwards, saw in Poe an expression of the new sensibility that they were themselves seeking. . . .'

It is scarcely surprising, then, that Debussy came early under his spell; and there were two tales in particular that haunted him throughout his life, *The Fall of the House of Usher* and *The*

[1] See Edward Lockspeiser: *Debussy: his life and mind*, Vol. I, p. 108, London 1962.
[2] Op. cit.

Devil in the Belfry. Both seemed to him to be ideal subjects for
an opera, but although he worked on and off at them all his life,
he never succeeded in finding for either the exact musical
transcription for which he was striving. He had nevertheless
drafted before he died a complete libretto for the *House of
Usher*, and had sketched substantial fragments of the music
which have been preserved in their unfinished state.[1] Frequent
allusions in his correspondence to both these works show the
extent to which he was obsessed by them, and one can only
regret that a project so dear to his heart was never realised. In
mood and substance, of course, the two stories are widely
different, the horror and morbid gloom of the *House of Usher*
being in vivid contrast to the ironic fantasy of the *Devil in the
Belfry*, a story similar in spirit to Stravinsky's *Histoire du soldat*.
Indeed, from Debussy's notes it would almost seem that the
music he projected might have had something in common with
Stravinsky's caustic score.... But this is perhaps to carry
speculation too far though, of course, we know in point of fact
that Stravinsky, especially in his early works, like every other
composer of his generation, owed more than a little to
Debussy.

The other most important literary influence which Debussy
was, inevitably, unable to escape was, of course, that of the
Symbolists; and it is significant that two of his most famous
works, the *Prélude à l'après-midi d'un Faune* and *Pelléas et
Mélisande* were directly inspired by the sympathy and admiration he felt for the two leading Symbolist poets of the day,
Stéphane Mallarmé and Maurice Maeterlinck. Mallarmé, to
whom he had been introduced by his literary friends, he knew
personally, and was one of the 'regulars' who attended the
poet's famous Tuesday gatherings at his apartment in the Rue
de Rome; with Maeterlinck his relations, amicable at first
when he obtained his permission to turn *Pelléas* into an opera,
later became strained, and ended in open hostility when the

[1] See Lockspeiser: *Debussy and Edgar Poe: Documents inédits*, Monaco 1962.

poet was offended because Debussy refused to cast his mistress in the role of Mélisande and gave the part to Mary Garden instead.

It was in 1892 that Debussy conceived the idea of writing a symphonic work directly inspired by a poem Mallarmé had written sixteen years previously describing, in what was almost a new language at the time, the daydream of a Faun drowsing in the noonday heat of some Mediterranean valley long ago, his sleep troubled by visions of amorous nymphs arousing him to an illusory pursuit ending in deception. Mallarmé's highly complex and elaborately constructed poem, full of verbal ingenuities in which syntax is sometimes strained to its limits, could not possibly, quite apart from its length, be 'set' in the ordinary way—although it is interesting to recall that an attempt had once been made (in 1887) to do just this by one Victor Emmanuele C. Lombardi, a musician belonging to an obscure sect calling itself *l'Ecole Evolutionniste-Instrumentiste* who had made a special cult of Mallarmé. In introducing his work which he called 'Glose' the composer spoke of 'following faithfully' the text, and had introduced a whole system of themes, or Leit-motifs, illustrating, almost bar by bar, the various images in the poem; and in the music accompanying the Faun's own narration of events (in contrast to his dreams), which Mallarmé prints in italics, he had even gone so far as to use a different typography in his score. The work had no success and little merit and, needless to say, was totally eclipsed by Debussy's triumphant version which succeeded precisely because it made *no* attempt to 'follow faithfully' the text. As he wrote to the critic Willy (Henri Gauthier-Villars): 'Perhaps my Prelude represents what remains of the Faun's dream in his flute. Or rather, it is a general impression of the poem, because if the music tried to follow it closely, it would soon be as out of breath as a cab-horse competing for the Grand Prix with a thoroughbred.' In another note, commenting on the work, Debussy defined his approach more precisely: 'The music of the *Prelude* is a very free illustration of Mallarmé's fine poem;

it does not in any way pretend to be a synthesis, but rather a succession of *décors* evoking the Faun's desires and dreams in the heat of that afternoon. Finally, tired of pursuing the nymphs and naiads in their timid flight, he abandons himself to intoxicating sleep, filled with dreams at last come true of total possession in universal Nature.'

The structure of Mallarmé's poem is extremely complex, employing every poetic device, as Valéry has pointed out, 'to express a threefold development of images and ideas, in which an extreme sensuality, an extreme intellectuality and an extreme musicality are combined, intermingled and opposed.' It has been suggested [1] that the theme of sensuality is represented by the rape of the nymphs; the musical theme being the transposition, in the Faun's memory and dreams, of the same episode which makes it clear that it was only a dream and not a reality; and finally the intellectual theme of Art, 'symbolized by the flute on which the Faun will preserve for eternity in his music the same dream, converting his illusion into an artistic reality.'

The poem is, indeed, a marvellous work of art, but owing to its esoteric language and extreme intellectuality might well have remained, as it were, a museum piece had not new life been breathed into it by Debussy, whose matchless music has ensured for *L'après-midi d'un Faune* an immortality it might not otherwise have attained.

At the time it was written it is no exaggeration to say that nothing quite like this music had been heard before. The orchestral texture alone was something quite new, as unlike Wagner as it was unlike that of any French composer of the period. There was nothing sensational or revolutionary about it, but the scoring is masterly in its discretion, the Faun's flute answered by murmurs from the muted horns in the opening bars, for example, with soft *glissandi* on the harps, creating at

[1] Suzanne Bernard: *Mallarmé et la musique*, Paris 1959.

one stroke the 'atmosphere', languid and dream-like of the whole poem—a perfect illustration of Verlaine's

> Oh! la nuance seule fiance
> le rêve au rêve et la flûte au cor.

The music has, too, a suppleness of contour and a fluidity new to French music, and is entirely free from those stereotyped developments to which the public's ear had become accustomed through listening to endless imitations of classical models. This fluidity of form was Debussy's great contribution to modern music and his own secret; and the *Faun* must be considered, if for this reason alone, a landmark in not only Debussy's own development but also in the history of Western music. The composer had already found himself, and found the language which he had been seeking since his student days.

It is worth recording that Mallarmé, not surprisingly in view of his 'jealousy' of music to which we have already alluded, was generally opposed to any 'settings' of his poems which he thought already contained their own music; and this was, in fact, what he said when he heard of Debussy's designs on *L'après-midi d'un Faune*. When he heard it, however, he was reconciled, and admitted that 'he had not expected anything like this. It is music that brings out the feeling of my poem, giving it a background warmer than colour.' And on the copy of his poem, which he presented to Debussy, he inscribed the following quatrain:

> Sylvain d'haleine première
> Si ta flûte a réussi
> Ouïs toute la lumière
> Qu'y soufflera Debussy.

thereby setting the seal of his approval on what he might have considered an incursion into his own domain.

An even more important landmark in Western music was the creation in 1902 of Debussy's only opera *Pelléas et Mélisande*, again the fruit of an intimate communion with the text of

another Symbolist poet, the Belgian Maurice Maeterlinck.
Debussy had been greatly impressed by the play when he first
read it in 1892, and still more so when he saw it the following
year in Lugné-Poé's production at the *Théâtre de l'Œuvre* in
Paris. It was then that he began seriously to compose the opera
with which his name will always be associated, and by 1895 he
had completed the first draft. This did not satisfy him, however, and he tore it up, because, as he explained to his friend the
composer Ernest Chausson, it showed too plainly the influence of Wagner; he was too conscious, when he looked at
what he had written, of 'the phantom of old Klingsor'. 'And
so', he wrote to Chausson, 'I am now seeking for a more personal idiom ('une petite chimie de phrases plus personnelles')
and am trying to be as much Pelléas as Mélisande. I have been
pursuing music, trying to penetrate behind all the accumula-
tion of veils by which she is shrouded from even her most
ardent devotees; and I have brought back something which
will please you, perhaps; I don't care about anyone else. I have
made use of a device which I think has very rarely been employed, namely silence (don't laugh!), as a means of expression
—and perhaps the only way to give emotional value to a
phrase. . . .' (Thus, in the love scene in Act IV the words 'je
t'aime', instead of being bawled out fortissimo in the most
approved operatic style, are murmured softly after all sound in
the orchestra had died away.)

Elsewhere Debussy speaks of the importance of 'preserving
intact the admirably symbolic qualities of music' ('les sym-
boles admirables de la musique'); and quite early in his career,
after his return from Bayreuth in 1889, he had told his friends
that he wanted to create a work in which 'music would take
over at the point at which words become powerless with the
one and only object of expressing that which nothing but
music could express. For this I need a text by a poet who, re-
sorting to discreet suggestion rather than to full statement, will
enable me to graft my dream upon his dream—who will give
me plain human beings in a setting belonging to no particular

period or place. . . . I do not wish my music to drown the words, nor to delay the course of action. I want no purely musical developments which are not called for inevitably in the text. In opera there is always too much singing. Music should be as swift and mobile as the words themselves.'

No wonder, then, that he found in Maeterlinck the perfect librettist, and was able to match the vague elusive speech and oppressive twilight atmosphere in which the characters move helplessly towards their inescapable destinies with music so perfectly in keeping. And yet, despite the rarified air they breathe and the extraordinary economy and reticence of the music that envelops them, we are somehow made to feel that these characters—the doomed lovers Pelléas and Mélisande, the jealous Golaud and Arkel, the wise old King who sees those around him being destroyed but, like the chorus in a Greek tragedy, can only make profound dispassionate comments on the frailty and capacity for suffering of the human heart—we are made to feel that they are all real human beings. Debussy, who lived with them for ten years, certainly thought of them as such, and involved himself in their joys and sorrows more deeply, perhaps, than a superficial listener might think. Had he not done so *Pelléas* would not be the profoundly moving work it is. An opera in which there are no set airs or *ensembles* and few, if any, opportunities for stage or vocal effects, and that seemed to run counter to every accepted tradition of 'grand opera' naturally shocked conservative opinion; and the first nights of *Pelléas* were marked by disgraceful scenes; although it seems clear that a cabal mounted against the composer by his enemies was partly, at least, responsible for what took place. His friends and admirers quickly rallied round, and after the first few nights the opera began to establish itself, and its rare qualities were soon not only recognised but approved by all discerning musicians.

Both in his treatment of the voices and of the orchestra Debussy broke entirely new ground. Mussorgsky's example, perhaps, caused him to pay special attention to the preservation

in the vocal line of the natural inflexions of the speaking
voice (a marvellous example of flawless accentuation is to be
found in the parlando style in the scene in the first act where
Geneviève, his mother, is reading Pelléas's letter beginning:
'Un soir je l'ai trouvée tout en pleurs au bord d'une fontaine');
but his orchestra is all his own, and the score abounds in all
kinds of subtle touches of colour and imaginative instrumental
grouping. The orchestra is never obtrusive, but invariably
eloquent. It does not comment; it reflects and illumines, rather
than underlines, the action on the stage. The vocal line is, for
the most part, in the nature of a *récitatif parlé*, or free declamation, though there are places, especially in the love scenes,
where the treatment of the voices is purely lyrical; and in certain scenes of passion and realism the music attains a high degree of more extrovert, but controlled, emotional intensity in
which effects of pity and horror are obtained with an absolute
economy of means and a laconic terseness which are immeasurably more impressive than any wild rhapsodic out-
burst could ever be. Debussy's whole aesthetic was largely
based on a hatred of emphasis and rhetoric, and its final and
supreme justification can be seen in *Pelléas*, the lyric drama that
will always be a landmark in the history of music, and of which
it might truthfully be said (as Cocteau said of the *Rite of Spring*)
that it opened and closed an epoch. Closed, because being inimitable it has had no direct successor; opened, because with it
modern music took a new turn, and the way was henceforth
open for the emancipation of opera as an art-form, thanks to
the discovery of an entirely new technique, the first-fruits of
which can be detected in, for example, such twentieth-
century music-dramas as the *Wozzeck* of Alban Berg.

There have, of course, been many lyric dramas since, but
never another *Pelléas*, although as an emancipating force, freeing operatic form from the mass of conventions and outworn
traditions it had gathered round it in the course of centuries,
its influence has been very great.

Turning now from this brief survey of the main literary influences which influenced Debussy as a young man and inspired him to write two of his best known masterpieces, it is time now to give some account of his career and of the other works which have ensured for him a very special place in musical history.

CHAPTER SIX

New horizons in music:
Debussy navigates uncharted seas

Writing in 1936, the French critic and essayist André Suarès in
his monograph on Debussy introduces his subject as follows:

'If today French music is, as it was in the lively Middle Ages
and stirring days of the first Renaissance, one of the brightest
jewels in Europe's crown, this is entirely due to Debussy. He
renovated whatever he touched: lyric song, keyboard music
and opera. In *Pelléas* he has left a model for all time for musicians aspiring to write for the theatre, and succeeded, where all
before him had failed, in achieving a perfect balance between
music and poetry in a work which nevertheless is wholly
musical. . . . Assuredly Debussy is the tree that overshadows
the whole forest; he is not in essence, unique; he has neigh-
bours and next-of-kin, just as he has roots: he is the product of
his people and of centuries; he represents a whole culture. . . .
Yet he has gone much farther than any school and escaped the
banal destiny of mere talent. He has that quality that has no
precedent, implied but undefined at any given moment: a
quality that transforms everything after it has been revealed,
though before it happened there was no reason to suppose
that it ever would. . . .'

One way of arriving at a fair and balanced estimation of
what Debussy really did achieve, and so of judging the extent
to which he may rightly be considered a seminal figure in the
evolution of twentieth-century music, would be to examine in
closer detail the claims made for him in the above quotation
and see how far they can be substantiated. Before doing so it is
necessary to look beyond the musician at the man and con-

sider for a moment the circumstances of his birth, upbringing, career and private life.[1]

I

Claude-Achille (or Achille-Claude as he appeared on his birth certificate) Debussy was born on 22 August 1862 in the little town of Saint-Germain-en-Laye, on the Western outskirts of Paris where his parents Manuel-Achille Debussy and his wife Victorine Josephine (née Manoury) kept a small china and hardware shop. He was the eldest of a family of five children, a sister and three brothers, all of whom survived him (except the youngest boy who died in infancy). Brought up in poverty and dependent on a thriftless and ineffectual father and a mother who seems, understandably, to have been somewhat lacking in any strong maternal feeling, the young Claude's childhood was not a happy one. Neither of his parents had any kind of cultural background, nor did any other member of his family show signs of possessing any special talent. It therefore remains one of the great miracles—and mysteries—in the history of the arts that by some freak of heredity such drab and undistinguished parents should have produced so great a genius as their eldest son turned out to be. Exactly how the boy's penchant for music first came to be discovered has never been satisfactorily explained, but the credit for giving him his first chance of developing the talent that was in him must go to a paternal aunt who, through her association with a wealthy and cultured man, was able to arrange for her nephew to have his first regular musical instruction in the form of piano lessons when he was six years old. It was chance again, and an even more incongruous and improbable chain of circumstances that enabled his father, thanks to the good offices of a companion-in-arms with whom he was fighting for the Commune in 1871, to speak of his son's now undoubted musical gift to

[1] Full details of these are of course available in any published *Life* of the composer, and will only be briefly recapitulated here.

this friend's mother who, besides being the mother-in-law of the poet Verlaine, was herself a well-known and distinguished pianist. Madame Antoinette Mauté de Fleurville, as she then was, after hearing the young Claude Debussy play, at once offered to give him piano lessons herself, and was so impressed by his precocious talent that, in spite of his tender age (he was barely ten at the time), she at once took steps to recommend him for admission to the Paris Conservatoire.

That he was able at that age to pass the very stiff entrance examination (in which only eight out of thirty-eight candidates were successful that year) is proof enough that this boy was more than ordinarily gifted; and from that moment his vocation was clear. The next ten years of his life were spent in the study of music, and from the first it was evident that he was going to be no ordinary pupil. In his harmony and composition classes he aired what seemed to his teachers to be revolutionary ideas, attacking all the accepted academic 'rules' and questioning their validity. Even his fellow-pupils were startled by his daring improvisations in which he introduced all kinds of novel and unheard-of chords and sequences which he justified on the grounds that they were pleasing to his ear. That was his only criterion. 'My rule', he said, 'is what I like.' Already he was in revolt against the conventional 'major-minor' scale; he wanted music to be free—to be a medium for the unfettered expression of feelings and sensations, and above all to reflect the vibrations of all the colours and sounds in Nature. And so, at this early age, he already knew what *kind* of music he wanted to write, and had his own ideas about what would have to be done to break down existing barriers and conventions by which music had for too long been oppressed. This did not, however, prevent him from acquiring a sound technique, and he was fortunate in having at least one professor, Ernest Guiraud, who understood him and gave him sympathetic encouragement.

His career at the Conservatoire was crowned by his winning the Grand Prix de Rome for composition with his cantata

L'Enfant Prodigue (in which, needless to say, he did not attempt to put into practice any of his revolutionary ideas); but the two years he had, as a consequence, to spend in Rome at the Villa Medici were, surprisingly, not a happy period in his life. While most young artists could be expected to consider themselves lucky to have three carefree years in Rome, Debussy was not only homesick, but in revolt against what he thought were the cramping restrictions of academic life in an official Institution. Accordingly he cut short his stay and returned to Paris at the end of two years.

This was not, however, the first time he had been abroad, for three years running, in the summer and autumn of the years 1880, 1881 and 1882, he had, while still a pupil at the Conservatoire, visited Russia and other parts of Europe as the pianist in a Trio of young musicians in the service of the lady who achieved fame as the wealthy patroness of Tchaikovsky, Madame von Meck. During these visits to Russia (Moscow and Mme von Meck's country estate at Brailov) he must have heard some contemporary Russian music, notably Borodine and certainly Tchaikovsky; but though an admirer of the former, he is unlikely to have been impressed by Tchaikovsky or to have had an opportunity to hear any of Mussorgsky's music, although in later life he was to develop a passion for this composer whose influence is discernible in some of his own works.

The years that followed Debussy's return from Rome to Paris at the age of twenty-five were an important formative period in his life. It was then that he made his first contacts with the literary and artistic world of Paris, meeting either at Edmond Bailly's *Librairie d'Art Indépendant*, then much frequented by the Symbolist writers and poets, or at Mallarmé's famous Tuesday gatherings in the Rue de Rome, artists like James McNeil Whistler and Odilon Redon, or such famous men of letters as Paul Verlaine, Henri de Régnier, Jules Laforgue, Villiers de l'Isle Adam and Pierre Louÿs. The latter was later to become one of Debussy's closest friends and, though nine years younger, was destined to play an important part in his life.

It was during these years, too, that Debussy had two major artistic experiences which left their mark upon him and influenced to some extent the formation of his musical style. In 1888 and 1889 he went to Bayreuth and heard for the first time *Parsifal, Tristan* and the *Mastersingers*; and in 1889, at the Great Exhibition in Paris, he had his first introduction to the music of the East, and was entirely subjugated by the simple, yet sophisticated beauties of the Javanese 'gamelan', memories of which remained with him all his life and undoubtedly had some influence on the formation of his mature style.

In the meantime he had formed a first more or less permanent liaison with Gabrielle Dupont (which was to last for some eight years); published his first settings of Verlaine and Baudelaire and completed *La Damoiselle élue*, a cantata for orchestra, female chorus and solo voices, based on a French translation of Dante Gabriel Rossetti's poem *The Blessed Damozel*.

By 1894 Debussy had 'arrived'; the revelation of the *Prélude à l'après-midi d'un Faune*, following that of the String Quartet, marked the dawn of a new epoch in not only French, but European music. The three *Nocturnes* (1898) established him as a master of a new style of iridescent orchestration, and four years later the production of *Pelléas et Mélisande* at the Opéra-Comique in Paris introduced, as we saw in the previous chapter, an entirely new concept of music-drama which has had far-reaching effects; for, by freeing operatic form from the mass of conventions and outworn traditions it had gathered round it in the course of centuries, Debussy in *Pelléas* virtually created at one stroke a new art-form, uniting music and drama in a way that had never been done before.

During the next five years *Pelléas* was produced in most of the European capitals, and Debussy was now an internationally famous composer, and began to accept engagements to conduct concerts of his music abroad. At home he continued to

Stéphane Mallarmé, 1841–1898

Claude Achille Debussy, 1862–1918

break new ground, enriching the orchestral repertoire with masterpieces like *La Mer* and the three *Images*, and writing some of his finest songs and piano music. *Estampes*, *L'Ile joyeuse* and the two sets of *Images* for piano belong to this period, as do the second set of *Fêtes galantes* and the *Trois chansons de Charles d'Orléans* for chorus *a cappella*.

Between 1910 and 1914 the major works were *Le Martyre de Saint Sébastien* (a mystery in five acts on a text by Gabriele d'Annunzio); the two Books of Preludes for the piano, the ballet *Jeux*, commissioned by Diaghilev and three of his finest sets of songs: *Le promenoir des deux amants*, *Trois Ballades de François Villon* and *Trois poèmes de Stéphane Mallarmé*.

Afflicted with an incurable cancer Debussy was by now a very sick man, and the horrors of the war added to his depression. Nevertheless by some miracle he was able to produce between 1914 and his death during the bombardment of Paris in 1918 some of his finest and most original music: the twelve Etudes for piano solo and *En blanc et noir* for two pianos, and the three great Sonatas for cello and piano, violin and piano, and flute, viola and harp.

He was twice married; once to Rosalie Texier ('Lilly') in 1899 after a tragic rupture with his former mistress Gabrielle; and *en secondes noces* to Emma Bardac in 1908 after a similarly tragic rupture with Lilly leading to his divorce in 1905. By his last wife he had a daughter, Claude-Emma ('Chouchou'), to whom he was, as also to her mother, passionately devoted. But Chouchou died from consumption at the age of fourteen, surviving her father by only one year.

II

What, then, are the qualities in the music of Debussy that have ensured for him a place among the great musicians of classical and modern times? Not merely the fact that, in the words of the critic quoted at the beginning of this chapter, 'he renovated whatever he touched', though that is true; it is rather because whatever he touched became transfigured and took on, as it were, a new dimension opening the way for the exploration of new and hitherto uncharted regions of human sensibility. Debussy's music, in fact, possesses that quality of unpredictableness of which our critic was thinking when he said that 'before it happened there was no reason to suppose that it ever would'. There have been many 'innovators' in the history of music, from Monteverdi to Stravinsky; the impact of Wagner alone on trends in Western music was very potent for a time, and so was that of Schoenberg. But in all these cases it would be possible to point to certain definable areas in which innovations were introduced: a new conception of the relations between words and music and a freer instrumental style was Monteverdi's contribution; Stravinsky disorganised the syntax of normal rhythm and Schoenberg that of harmony; while Wagner prepared the way for both if only by providing them with a target against which to react by his cult of the colossal and the sublime.

With Debussy it was very different. He had no axe to grind, no 'system' to impose and no desire at all to be considered a revolutionary. His greatest innovations, perhaps, were to conceive of music as being basically ἁρμονία, an art of sounds considered in combination (vertically) rather than in extension (horizontally), and to repudiate the idea of stereotyped forms into which music must be poured as a cook pours her various ingredients into different moulds. Yet it would be a great mistake to think of his music as being formless. On the contrary, every thought he put on paper was shaped by a rigid inner necessity which dictated the placing of every accent and every nuance of harmony and rhythm; and each work demanded its own special form, as inseparable from its inner content as the fur or feathers on an animal or bird are from the bodies they envelop. Debussy was also perhaps the first composer in whose hands harmony becomes melody. Thus, in a sequence of shifting harmonies the melody sometimes can be found, not so much in the outer parts as in the inner, as they melt and merge one into the other. This conception of harmonic melody is one of Debussy's greatest innovations, and invests much of his music with a very special kind of aura which makes it unlike any other. Already in his student days at the Conservatoire he was in revolt against the conventional musical language of the nineteenth century, with its diatonic scale and endless dominant-to-tonic cadences, and sought (in a different way from Wagner who pushed chromaticism to its furthest limits to escape from the same tyranny) to free music from what he felt were artificial restrictions by making it more flexible and enriching its somewhat worn-out vocabulary. This he did, in the first place, by largely replacing the standard diatonic 'major-minor' scale by others based on the ancient 'modes' or, like the whole-tone and pentatonic scales, borrowed from the East. In this way he opened the door to those unconventional harmonies which give to his music that characteristic tonal fluidity and even ambiguity which are among its greatest charms, and of which he alone possessed the secret. To be able to travel from one tonality to another freely without having recourse to conventional 'modulations' was his main aim; and when he spoke of 'drowning tonality' ('noyer le ton' was the expression he used) he did not mean abolish it, but, rather, soften and blur its outlines and thus make it possible to pass almost imperceptibly from one 'key' to another without unduly emphasizing any particular one. (It is significant in this context that with the solitary exception of the String Quartet 'in G minor', no work of Debussy has any key label attached to it. Indeed, there are passages in some of the later works, e.g., the twelve Etudes for piano, which are to all intents and purposes atonal.)

Another of Debussy's paradoxical innovations was his rediscovery of the 'common chord', and revolutionary use of consonances to create an atmospheric and sometimes archaic effect; instances abound in *Pelléas*, and notably in the settings of Villon's *Ballades*. In the same way, he used sequences of unprepared and unresolved 'discords' (e.g., consecutive 'Ninths' and 'Elevenths') as if they were consonances to great effect; this procedure is one of Debussy's most characteristic 'finger-prints'—but, incidentally, one which had already been practised to some extent by both Chabrier and Satie. The important thing to remember is that all Debussy's innovations had an aesthetic *raison d'être*. He had no desire to 'revolutionise' music (did he not say on one occasion: 'Heureusement, nous ne sommes pas modernes . . . ma musique n'est pas faite pour d'autres buts: se mêler aux âmes et choses de bonne volonté'); his one aim was to express the inexpressible—'l'Inexprimable qui est l'Idéal de tout art'—by means of music—that music which for him was 'a dream unveiled': 'La musique, c'est du rêve dont on écarte les voiles.'

Fortunately, from a technical point of view his craftsman-ship was equal to his exacting standards of perfection, and no composer ever had a finer ear for the ultimate refinements of orchestral and pianistic sonorities; his mastery in these two fields is complete and unquestioned.

Already in *L'après-midi d'un Faune* he was making the orchestra sound as it had never sounded before in the hands of any French, German or Russian composer of the period, owing nothing, for example, to either Wagner, Rimsky-Korsakov or Richard Strauss—generally considered the greatest masters in this particular field at that time. In the Nocturnes again (*Nuages, Fêtes, Sirènes*), perhaps the only work of Debussy's that could fairly be described as 'Impressionist', his handling of the orchestra is quite remarkable. From beginning to end the instrumentation is miraculous; the palette rich and subtle, and full of inventive and imaginative touches, from the delicate brushwork of the solemnly drifting clouds in *Nuages* through the 'dazzling, fantastic vision' (Debussy's own words) of the procession in *Fêtes* to the final tableau, *Sirènes*, where an unseen choir of women's voices is used with magical effect.

In *La Mer* Debussy revealed another side of his genius which somewhat disconcerted his critics and admirers; they were not prepared for so robust and full-blooded a work, so solidly constructed, so positive and unambiguous. It is the only one of Debussy's works that could be described as a 'Tone Poem', although it is also almost the only one to be cast in classical form, each of the three sketches of which it is composed corresponding to the movements of a symphony or concerto—Allegro, Scherzo and Finale—while the individual sections show traces of something very like sonata form. As descriptive music, depicting various aspects of the sea, for which Debussy had a lifelong passion as one of the supreme manifestations of Nature, it has never been surpassed; but it is also the only example in his entire *œuvre* of what could be called a piece of solid symphonic writing. Like all true creative artists he had no wish to go on repeating himself indefinitely, and in his next, and last, purely orchestral work, the highly-wrought and elaborate, though still partially pictorial, *Images* (*Ibéria, Gigues, Rondes de Printemps*), he composed a triptych of three contrasting panels—a highly coloured evocation of Spain; an ironic and melancholy fantasia on the English North country folk tune the *Keel Row;* and a delicate Pastorale depicting May-day festivities in which much use is made of the old French tune 'Nous n'irons plus au bois'. Just as many admirers of Stravinsky were disappointed that after the *Rite of Spring* he changed his style, so did Debussy disconcert the 'Debussy-istes' who were just getting used to the idiom of *Pelléas* by his determination to pursue his goal of a completely emancipated musical language to the end. Hence the marked stylistic differences to be observed in each major work. *The Martyre de Saint-Sébastien*, his only attempt at religious drama, differs as much from *La Mer* as the late piano works (notably the twelve Etudes) and Sonatas do from works of his middle period—such as the *Images* and the two books of Piano Preludes.

The composition of the *Saint Sébastien* music was undertaken in such strange circumstances that they are worth recalling. One of Debussy's most fervent admirers was the Italian poet-adventurer, the notorious Gabriele d'Annunzio, who had bestowed upon his favourite composer the title of 'Claude de France'. In 1911 he quite unexpectedly invited Debussy to compose some incidental music for his own Mystery play *The Martyrdom of Saint Sebastian* at very short notice; and Debussy was so anxious to accept the challenge that, contrary to his custom, he agreed to the time limit and produced his score in a matter of months. He was so pressed for time, however, that he had to entrust part of the orchestration to his friend and disciple André Caplet who was going to conduct the performance.

D'Annunzio described his five-act play as a 'lyrical glorification, not only of this splendid Christian athlete (Saint Sebastian) but also of all Christian heroism.' Nevertheless it was banned by the Church, and Catholics were forbidden by the Archbishop of Paris to attend performances. This was on account of the semi-pagan and excessively sensual treatment of the Martyrdom in which the worship of Adonis is confounded with the cult of Christ. To make matters worse the part of the Saint was to be mimed by the Jewish dancer Ida Rubinstein.

It was probably the pagan element in the piece that appealed to Debussy as a pantheist; and in an interview published at the time he declared that, while he did not practise religion in accordance with the sacred rites, 'I have made mysterious Nature my religion. . . . Nature in all her grandeur is truthfully reflected in my soul . . . is it not then obvious that a man who sees mystery in everything will inevitably be attracted to a religious subject? I can assure you that I wrote my music as if I had been asked to do it for a church. The result is decorative music. . . . Is the faith it expresses orthodox or not? I cannot say. It is my own faith, singing in all sincerity.'

This is one of the rare statements made by Debussy with regard to religion, though he was known to hold the view that there had been no genuine sacred music since the sixteenth century, when 'the beautiful child-like souls of those days were alone capable of expressing their passionate disinterested fervour in music free from all worldliness'. This conviction dates back to his student days at the Villa Medici when he had been very impressed by the music of Palestrina and Orlando de Lassus which he had heard in Roman churches; and it was this experience that led him to declare that this was the only kind of church music he could accept: 'That of Gounod and Co. appears to be the product of an hysterical mysticism, and seems no better than a sinister farce.'

The *Martyre* has never been a success owing to its hybrid nature which makes it impossible to produce on the stage either as a ballet or an operatic cantata or as a mixture of both. Nevertheless, in spite of the speed with which it was written it contains some remarkable music, some of it unlike anything Debussy had ever written before. The exultant choruses, big climaxes and general richness of texture and firm outlines of both the choral and orchestral writing reveal a Debussy very different from the composer of the *Faun* or *Pelléas*. The inspiration may not be sustained throughout (incidental music must always be more or less subservient to the drama it accompanies), but in it, Debussy, with his usual sensitive response to the full implications of a literary text, caught exactly the right note of semi-mystical, semi-erotic fervour with which d'Annunzio's 'Mystery' is impregnated, and the score of *Le Martyre* contains some memorable pages.

As in every other field, Debussy enormously enriched the singer's repertory, and there has been no greater master of that specifically French song-form, the *mélodie*—a genre for which he was particularly well equipped owing to the fineness of his ear and his exceptional sensitivity to modern poetry which made him the ideal interpreter in sound of poets like Verlaine, Baudelaire and Mallarmé. From the earliest settings of Verlaine—the *Ariettes oubliées* and *Fêtes Galantes* (1st series)— and of Baudelaire—the *Cinq poèmes*—through the *Proses lyriques*, for which he wrote his own rather precious verses to music already precociously rich and rare, the delightful *Chansons de Bilitis* and the haunting second series of *Fêtes galantes* to the exquisite *Promenoir des deux amants*, the noble *Ballades de*

François Villon and the elegantly sophisticated *Trois poèmes de Stéphane Mallarmé*, the last of the great song-cycles, we are conscious of the same fine sensibility and poetic insight, becoming more rarified towards the end, but always supremely musical.

The specifically French *mélodie*, lying somewhere between the *chanson* and the German *Lied*, is not so much a *song* in the ordinary sense of the word, as a re-creation in musical terms of both the sound and spirit of a poem—less 'serious', less 'moral', more pictorial than the *Lied*, and differing from the *chanson* (which is more or less independent of its words, being basically a 'tune' in its own right) by reason of its extreme fluidity and sometimes, paradoxically, its lack of 'melody'. Thus in Debussy's setting of Verlaine's *Colloque sentimentale*, for example, there is virtually no vocal 'line'; while the singer murmurs the words charged with emotion, it is left to the piano to convey the tense and ghostly atmosphere in a succession of skilfully placed brush-strokes, as it were, of harmonic colour. The poem is simply reborn in terms of music.

Debussy's contribution to the literature of the piano is also outstanding; he did for the twentieth century what Chopin did for the nineteenth—endowed the piano with a new voice and created for it some matchless music which has in some respects revolutionised pianistic technique and enormously extended the instrument's potentialities. Unlike the modern school of composers who tend to use the piano as a percussive instrument, Debussy was interested primarily in its harmonic possibilities—as an instrument capable of blending and sustaining, by means of the pedal, shifting harmonies contained in sequences of carefully spaced chords. He aimed at a kind of transparent sonority which could be obtained by attacking a note in a certain way, without force, and then prolonging the sound with the pedal after lifting the finger from the key. He used to tell his pupils to forget that the piano has hammers, and encouraged them to caress rather than strike the keys with their fingers—or, as the late Marguerite Long, who was his pupil, remembered him saying: to make their hands 'entrer dedans'

—get *inside* the piano, rather than strike it from above. And so he used to teach his pupils to play chords by making the keys 'rise towards their finger-tips as if attracted by a magnet'.

Because the pedal plays a very important part in the correct interpretation of so much of his piano music, a complete mastery of pedal technique is indispensable to the pianist who aspires to play his music. One characteristic device of which he was very fond is that known as 'half-pedalling', employed for a special colour effect. The device consists of raising the dampers by depressing the 'loud' pedal, and then allowing them to come in contact for a fraction of a second with the vibrating string by half releasing the pedal and then immediately depressing it again. Debussy's own style of piano playing was the embodiment of what he taught. Like Chopin, who had greatly influenced his first teacher, Mme de Fleurville, and of all composers the one for whom he professed unbounded admiration, Debussy rarely employed a fortissimo, or even a forte when he played. His tone was usually veiled and on one occasion when he appeared in public to perform, towards the end of his life, one critic wrote that his pianissimo was continuous and, at times, almost inaudible.

The key to a proper understanding of Debussy's attitude towards the piano is to realise that he wanted more than anything to make the piano second only to the orchestra as a vehicle for hitherto undreamed of effects of atmosphere and colour, and rare and poignant sonorities. Chopin and Liszt had already greatly extended the possibilities of the piano from the point of view of both expression and technique: Liszt through the cultivation of pure virtuosity, and Chopin by endowing the instrument with a soul and treating it as a singing voice. But it was left to Debussy to open the door still wider to both poetry and virtuosity; and it is the combination of these qualities, plus an indefinable 'something'—perhaps a touch of irony here and there, but above all a determination to make the strings of the piano vibrate with all the colours of the orchestra—that give to Debussy's keyboard music its unique and unmistakable character.

It is a far cry from the *Arabesques* and *Petite Suite* of 1888/9 to the *Douze Etudes* of 1915; but that quarter of a century represents a new epoch in the history of the piano, during which its repertory and resources were so enriched and extended by Debussy (and also by Ravel) that their innovations have had a lasting influence on all twentieth-century composers writing for the instrument.

Debussy was a slow developer, and between his earliest and latest works for the piano the difference in style and content is very marked. After the mellifluous *Suite Bergamasque* (1890) the style begins to harden in *Pour le Piano*, and a definite turning-point is reached with the *Estampes* of 1903 where, for the first time, an exotic element is deliberately introduced, with echoes of the Javanese *gamelang* in *Pagodes*, and of Spanish rhythms in *La soirée dans Grenade*. But it is in the two sets of *Images* and the two books of twelve Preludes that some of the finest and rarest gems of Debussy's pianistic inspiration will be found.

In the six *Images*—*Reflets dans l'eau, Hommage à Rameau* and *Mouvement* (1905) and *Cloches à travers les feuilles, Et la lune descend sur le temple qui fut* and *Poissons d'or* (1907)—we find all the characteristics of Debussy's 'middle period', namely increasingly rarified harmonies, absence of superfluous trimmings, a studied preoccupation with the spacing of chords and the most careful cultivation of purely pianistic sonorities. The titles are sometimes cited as evidence of Debussy's preciosity, but in reality he was only observing an old French custom and carrying on the tradition of the seventeenth- and eighteenth-century *clavecinistes* who invariably gave fanciful titles to their keyboard pieces: Couperin le Grand is an obvious example. *Poissons d'or* is said to have been inspired by a Japanese lacquer tray or screen depicting gold-fish; but in the case of *Cloches à travers les feuilles* the title was suggested to the composer by his friend and biographer, Louis Laloy, who wrote from the country, where he was prolonging his stay into late autumn, telling of the local custom of tolling the church bells at Hallowe'en, and the mysteriously beautiful effect of the sound of bells heard in the evening through the silent forest. Laloy, who was a Chinese scholar and an authority on Oriental art, was also probably responsible for the title *Et la lune descend sur le temple qui fut*, which is a most delicate evocation of a Far-Eastern landscape in which, to quote Laloy, 'the music . . . is like a translucid precious stone, born of space and silence'.

The twelve *Préludes* in the first Book are remarkable for their conciseness and expressive, sometimes purely pictorial qualities. Each one carries a more or less literary title (very characteristic of Debussy) which is, however, placed at the end and not at the beginning of each piece, as if to suggest that the title was an afterthought, and not the source of inspiration. Well-known examples are *La cathédrale engloutie* (the cathedral which according to the old Breton legend lies buried under the waves at Ys); *La fille aux cheveux de lin* (a Pre-Raphaelite-like portrait of a girl with flaxen hair); impressions of sailing-boats at anchor (*Voiles*); of a hurricane (*Ce qu'a vu le vent de l'Ouest*); and an evocation of all that is implied in Baudelaire's celebrated line: 'Les sons et les parfums tournent dans l'air du soir.'

It is noticeable, however, that in none of these is the pictorial element unduly stressed if stressed at all; these Preludes are pure music and among the most imaginative and sensitive works in the whole literature of the piano.

In the second book of *Préludes*, published in 1913, the tendency to preciosity is perhaps more marked, and the humor, supposedly Anglo-Saxon, in *General Lavine, eccentric*, and *Hommage à S. Pickwick Esq.* is somewhat laboured. But the exquisite *Canope*, with its subtle semitonal *frottements* (suggesting that Debussy would have welcomed a microtonal keyboard); the vivid and authentically Hispanic *Puerta del Vino* (admired by Falla); and *"Les fées sont d'exquises danseuses"* (inspired by Arthur Rackham's illustration of a sentence in J. M. Barrie's *Peter Pan in Kensington Gardens*), are pianistic gems. Finally, the literally dazzling virtuosity of *Feux d'artifice*,

with which the series ends, reveals the composer in yet another
light: as the *bouquet* explodes in the sky, Debussy ironically
dismisses us with a faraway echo of the *Marseillaise*.

Taken together, the Twenty-four Preludes may be said to
mark the end of a phase in Debussy's development; he was
now about to embark on his 'last period' which was productive of several master works, all produced during the 1914 war
when he was physically weakened by illness, but mentally alert
and full of ideas about the future of music.

The war was a great shock to Debussy. While it exacerbated
his patriotic sentiments, it increased his consciousness of being
a useless member of society and made it more and more difficult for him to work. For a long time he was almost incapable
of putting pen to paper. In a letter to his publisher and friend,
Jacques Durand, he compared himself to 'a poor atom buffeted
by this terrible cataclysm; what I am doing seems to me so
miserably small. . . . Claude Debussy, if he's not making music
has no reason for existing. . . .'

But gradually his thoughts turned to music again, and his
main concern at the moment being the necessity, as he saw it,
of safeguarding French culture against the rising ride of bar-
barism. Thus, in January 1915, he wrote to Dr. Pasteur
Valléry-Radot: 'I have begun again to write a little music,
mostly so as not to forget it completely, very little for my own
satisfaction. . . . It seems to me there is an opportunity of re-
verting not to a too narrow and contemporary French tradition,
but to the real one which one can place immediately after
Rameau—just when it was beginning to be lost! Shall we have
the courage? Shall we dare to extricate from the depths which
have gradually been engulfing it the true French clarity?'

Here we have the key to Debussy's 'last period' works
which at one time it had been the fashion to underrate. Some
critics saw in them signs of waning powers and enfeebled
invention; but is not this largely because they expected something else, something more familiar? Having grown accustomed to Fauns and Gardens in the rain and the twilight world

of *Pelléas et Mélisande*, to moonlight and drifting clouds, they felt ill at ease in bright daylight, when shadows are clearcut and outlines sharp and distinct. And so there was a time when the three last Sonatas and the great Etudes for piano, in which Debussy was so obviously seeking to purify his style and bring it more into line with the great French tradition going back to the sixteenth and seventeenth centuries, were judged inferior to his earlier work. What his critics failed to see was that it was not only a question of going back, but of looking forward too; for these last works may be considered as, in a sense, fore-runners of the 'new', more abstract music which came into being in the third decade of this century. Debussy himself un-doubtedly took this view, for only three years before his death he wrote to Valléry-Radot: 'I have still so much to say. There are so many things in music which have never yet been done—for example, the human voice—I don't think it has ever up to now been fully exploited' ('on ne lui a pas encore fait rendre tout ce qu'elle pouvait'). These are not the words of an artist who has run short of ideas.

It is true he wrote no more for the voice—his life was running out and time was short—but in spite of his illness and anxiety about the war he was yet, by some miracle, able to com-pose the twelve Etudes which occupy a unique and memorable place in the entire literature of the piano. Written only three years before he died, they show that tightening of the sinews, that tendency towards a greater concision that characterise all his later works. The picturesque and sensuous elements are notably less prominent than in the earlier piano works, but the demands made upon the player's virtuosity are extremely exacting. Between them the twelve studies cover a wide field, each one being devoted to a different theme, musical as much as technical, some exploiting the possibilities of writing in thirds and fourths and sixths and octaves, others using orna-ments, repeated notes, chromatic intervals, arpeggios and what Debussy calls 'sonorités opposées' (this is a beautifully subtle study in harmonic contrasts) as the main themes in a series of

masterly essays in virtuosity. But these Etudes are more than
that; they are all, without exception, miracles of abstract
musical creation, reflecting no less clearly than those of Chopin
(to whose memory they are dedicated), despite the difference of
idiom, the subtly working and inventive mind of a great and
sensitive musician.

The Sonata for cello and piano (one of Debussy's most perfect achievements) written immediately after the Etudes was
the first of a planned series of six sonatas for different combinations of instruments which were intended by the composer to
be a manifestation of his belief in the necessity of keeping alive
the classic French tradition which he felt was being threatened
by unwholesome foreign influences; and to mark this new
patriotic, or rather nationalist outlook, he deliberately added
to his ordinary signature, Claude Debussy, the words: 'musicien français'. The second sonata is for flute (originally oboe),
viola and harp; the third for violin and piano. The remaining
three were never written, but the fourth was to have been for
oboe, horn and harpsichord (as noted on the manuscript of the
third sonata).

The impetuosity of the Violin Sonata, the fantasy and way-
wardness of the Cello Sonata (which is conceived in the spirit
of the Italian *commedia dell' arte*) and the ornamental and rhythmic complexities of the Trio, to say nothing of the new note of
harmonic austerity and 'bareness' so noticeable in all three, give
to these works a special character of their own and show the
composer in a new light. They are, of course, almost the only
works that have no literary or extra-musical content; and it is
significant that at the end of his life he should have started to
concentrate on abstract music for the first time. For in these
sonatas are the germs of the neo-classical movement that was to
flourish after the first world war; and this leads us inevitably
to speculate as to the kind of music Debussy might have
written had he lived on into the 'twenties and early 'thirties.

It is in any case remarkable that a sick man, however great
his genius, could have produced these admirably lucid works

which bear so little trace of the circumstances in which they were conceived. Debussy himself (in a letter to his friend the critic and essayist Robert Godet) remarked in his usual vein of bantering irony, that the Violin Sonata would be interesting 'from a documentary point of view and as an example of what a sick man can write in time of war'; but at the same time he pointed out that the mood of the whole work was in striking contrast with his own at the time it was composed, being 'full of life, almost joyous'. And this prompted him to ask whether this is not a proof of how little a man's own feelings are concerned with what is occupying his brain ('du peu que nous sommes dans les aventures où s'engage notre cerveau. L'esprit souffle où il veut').

Debussy even found strength to play the piano part of this sonata at a concert in Paris in May 1917; but this was his last public appearance, and a year later, on 25 March 1918, he died in Paris while the city was being bombarded by German bombs, and shells from their long-range cannon. A strange and tragic irony had ordained that the composer who knew so well the value of silence in his life and work should be condemned to die surrounded by the din and turmoil of a dreadful war.

Owing to the war very few tributes to the great composer who had just passed away appeared in the French press, though abroad the sad event was the occasion of laudatory articles in many languages. One of the most apposite private tributes came from the writer P. J. Toulet (who had collaborated with Debussy over a projected opera on *As you like it*). In a letter to Pasteur Valléry-Radot, Toulet wrote: 'Et je ne vous dis rien—car il y en aurait trop à dire—de ce que m'inspire cette mort du point de vue de l'art français dont il représente si parfaitement, par sa musique, ces claires profondeurs qui semblent emprun-tées de la mer.'[1]

---

[1] 'I can't tell you—because there would be too much to tell—what an impression his death has made on me, especially in regard to French art of which he represents so perfectly in his music that transparent profundity that seems to have been borrowed from the sea. . . .'

CHAPTER SEVEN

RAVEL, SATIE, 'LES SIX':
CLOSER LINKS BETWEEN MUSIC AND LETTERS

The years 1931–37 marked the end of an important era in the history of modern French music. For within that short period died four of the last great composers who had been Debussy's contemporaries, but, unlike him, had lived on after the first world war: Vincent d'Indy, Paul Dukas, Albert Roussel and Maurice Ravel; only Charles Koechlin lived to see the second war, dying in 1950 at the age of eighty-three.

Of these, the nearest in some ways to Debussy, in so far as he can be considered a key figure in the evolution of 'modern' French music, though differing in so many others, was Maurice Ravel. Though born thirteen years after Debussy, he reached his musical maturity far more quickly, and had written many of his best works before Debussy had really found himself. He was sixty-two when he died; but during the last five years of his life an obscure nervous disease, caused by pressure on an artery in the brain, had affected his mental faculties and made it impossible for him to compose—or even to sign his name. No more tragic affliction could have come upon a musician whose exceptionally keen intellect and rare sensitivity is reflected in everything he wrote. For Ravel was one of the most consummate musical craftsmen the world has ever known. His technical virtuosity was prodigious; and his music, in whatever medium he was working, whether piano, orchestra, operatic or instrumental, is as finely wrought as any of those exquisite Chinese or Japanese *objets d'art* which he admired so passionately and with which he adorned his country house at Montfort l'Amaury. The word that can be applied more fittingly than any other to Ravel, both as a man and as an artist, is

Maurice Ravel, 1875–1937

Erik Satie, 1866–1925

fastidious. He was as fastidious in his tastes, in his dress and in his choice of friends as he was in his music; and so far from wearing his heart upon his sleeve, he hid it so successfully that there are those who affirm he was born without one. It is true that there is about his music, as there was in his physical presence and comportment, a certain cold detachment and aloofness, a shrinking from any overt manifestation of emotion of any kind; but this extreme reserve, reflected in his character no less than in his art, was probably to some extent a mask. He said once to a friend: 'People are always saying I have no heart. It is not true. But I am a Basque, and the Basques feel things very strongly, but rarely reveal their feelings, and then only to a very few.' At the same time it is undeniable that no other composer of his stature has ever quite so deliberately made a cult of artificiality, or so persistently excluded from his music any intrusion of his own personality; the last thing he wanted to do was 'express himself'. For him, music was a kind of ritual, having its own laws, to be conducted behind high walls, within a kind of magic circle, sealed off from the outside world and impenetrable to unauthorized intruders. In the act of creation nothing extraneous to the music itself could be tolerated, and above all, no whiff of human passion. Ravel would not perhaps have denied that these exist, but there was no place for them in his music. Hence his cult of artificiality and pastiche, and the attraction he always felt for mechanical toys, automata, puppets and inanimate objects in general. Even in his operas he was careful to choose subjects which would not involve him in the portrayal of any 'dramatic' or emotional human situations (without which most operatic composers would be lost) but provide him, on the contrary, merely with opportunities for humour, irony or satire. Thus the plot of *L'Heure Espagnole* relieved him of having to treat his characters as anything other than puppets; for what appealed to him most in Franc-Nohain's satirical comedy was its artificiality, verbal conceits and equivocal situations, and the opportunites which its setting—a clockmaker's shop in eighteenth-century Toledo

—offered him in the way of pastiche local colour, and realistic imitations of ticking clocks, and the whirring and creaking of mechanical toys. He even succeeded in dehumanizing completely the already distinctly artificial characters in the comedy and reducing them to the stature of marionettes. Similar opportunities were afforded him in his only other operatic venture, *L'Enfant et les sortilèges*, the fairy story Colette had written for her small daughter, where Ravel is once again completely in his element among the humanized animals, talking clocks and teapots and waltzing furniture. But here, in this work of his maturity, are signs, almost for the first time, of real human feeling and even pathos—as in the child's address to the Fairy Princess 'Toi, le cœur de la rose...', the episode of the wounded squirrel and the child's last appeal to his mother where the two syllables 'Maman', pronounced as a falling fourth (a characteristic Ravelian fingerprint) strike an almost sentimental note which psychologists might perhaps interpret as one of the rare expressions in his music of Ravel's undoubted 'mother-fixation' which remained with him all his life.

It is possible, of course, to make too much of what Roland-Manuel once called Ravel's '*esthétique de l'imposture*', suggesting that, for him, 'art is not the supreme truth, but rather the most dazzling lie—a marvellous imposture'. Nevertheless, it is on record that the composer, tired of hearing these accusations of artificiality, once protested: 'How do they know I am not artificial by nature?' In any evaluation of Ravel this remark must always be borne in mind, but need in no way lessen our enjoyment of his music. Such works as the early but perfect String Quartet, the charming piano Sonatine and the *Mother Goose* suite appeal equally to the ordinary music lover and the connoisseur; while the big piano works, like *Gaspard de la nuit*, *Jeux d'eau*, *Miroirs*, with its brilliant *Alborado*, and above all the subtle and evocative *Valses nobles et sentimentales*, seem to contain the quintessence of Ravel's very individual brand of sophisticated sensitivity.

His mastery of the orchestra and the richness of his instrumental palette can be seen again in the *Rapsodie espagnole*, the ballet *Daphnis et Chloë*, *La Valse* and *Bolero* (intended deliberately to be a *tour de force*); while in the two Piano Concertos, especially the one for the Left Hand, with its tragic undertones and haunting use of jazz rhythms, Ravel has enriched the pianist's repertoire with undoubted masterpieces.

Maurice Ravel was born at Ciboure, a little fishing-port between St. Jean-de-Luz and the Spanish frontier, on 7 March 1875. He was of mixed Swiss-Basque descent, his father, Pierre-Joseph Ravel being a distinguished engineer, while his mother, *née* Marie Deluart, came from a Spanish-Basque family. It may seem paradoxical that the musician, who, of all others, is generally considered to be the most typically French, should thus have been of mixed Swiss and Basque descent; but this is the kind of paradox that seems inseparable from everything connected with Ravel, with just enough of that element of unreality which he cultivated so assiduously in his art and sought for in his life.

The contribution he made to French music was different in kind from that of Debussy; and despite certain superficial resemblances, the two men, so far as methods, technique and above all temperament are concerned, had very little in common. At one time Ravel was accused (notably by Pierre Lalo, music critic of *Le Temps*) of being unduly 'influenced' by Debussy; but there is no real evidence to support this, though Ravel never concealed the great admiration he felt for Debussy, and indeed on one occasion paid him the greatest compliment one composer could pay to another when he confessed that it was when he heard for the first time *L'Après-midi d'un Faune* that he understood 'what music was about' ('ce qu'était la musique'). Debussy, for his part was more grudging in his recognition of Ravel's great qualities, though he did once declare (à propos of the *Valses nobles et sentimentales*) that Ravel's ear was the 'finest in the world'. ('C'est l'oreille la plus fine qui ait jamais existé.')

Such rivalry as there was between the two musicians was largely fomented not so much by themselves (if at all) but by their respective partisans representing the various schools of musical thought that were very active at that time. As to resemblances between them, these, at best, were only superficial —e.g., a partiality for chords of the ninth and eleventh, and for modal rather than diatonic cadences—and that Ravel was conscious of this is shown by a remark he once made to a critic to the effect that any likeness between his music and Debussy's was due, not to any 'influence', but to what he called an 'innate resemblance' (similitude innée). It is clear, however, that this 'resemblance' applies far more to their general aesthetic outlook and literary tastes—both for example admired Mallarmé, Baudelaire and Poe, and both had a taste for rare and precious sensations—than to their methods or style of composition. The classicism of Ravel's form and his clearly defined and precise outlines are in marked contrast to Debussy's far more fluid structures and atmospheric harmonies; and whereas Ravel did not mind if his 'scaffolding' was visible, Debussy was always anxious that his music should sound like an improvisation. Temperamentally they were poles apart, Debussy for example, being a pantheist and a devotee of Nature, while Ravel delighted in artifice and preferred his emotions second-hand. Darius Milhaud, who knew them both, contrasts Debussy's 'human qualities' ('everything came from his heart') with Ravel's 'preciosity'; and though this may be a 'subjective' reaction, it is nevertheless one that underlines the essential difference between the two composers. Debussy, in fact, inhabited a different world—a world into which Ravel did not seek to penetrate; but the co-existence and contemporaneity of two such outstanding musicians not unnaturally led to various misunderstandings and misjudgments which with the passage of time can now be seen in their right perspective.

Ravel was above all a consummate craftsman, and without being in any sense revolutionary, he was very much abreast of his time and keenly interested in the 'new' music of Schoenberg and Stravinsky from a purely technical point of view. After studying the score of *The Rite of Spring* with its composer he wrote to his friends urging them not to miss its first performance which he was convinced would be 'as important an event as the première of *Pelléas*'. He was also impressed by Schoenberg's *Pierrot Lunaire*, and admitted that he had this work in mind when composing his *Trois poèmes de Mallarmé*, the instrumentation of which is almost identical with that of *Pierrot Lunaire*. It is true that he had no desire to disrupt either the grammar or the syntax of music, as Schoenberg and Stravinsky seemed at that time to be doing, and was content to work in classical forms and on the basis of the generally accepted harmonic system of his day, still firmly rooted in tonality. At the same time there is no doubt that he did extend that basis very considerably, and enriched the harmonic language derived from it in a way that seemed at the time both original and bold. Indeed, so very personal and individual was his adaptation and manipulation of the traditional nineteenth-century musical idiom as taught in the Conservatories that it could almost be said that he created a language of his own. Ravel saw what diatonic harmony was potentially capable of; and being endowed with an extremely acute ear and a taste for rare and subtle harmonies, he evolved a style which bears the stamp of his personality as unmistakably as any page of Bach or Chopin. He rarely uses the ordinary classical major-minor scale, and always avoids the 'leading note'; but while Debussy had a preference for chords of the ninth and the whole-tone scale, Ravel cultivated the eleventh harmonic and never employed the whole-tone scale. His melodies are almost invariably modal, the modes he uses most frequently being the Dorian (d–d¹) and the Phrygian (e–e¹), the latter being characteristic of Andalucian folk-music and the former of Basque music. While his harmonies sometimes appear to be extremely *recherchés* and even disconcerting, they will generally be found to be composed of chords of the seventh, ninth and eleventh, but variously disguised, often with unresolved appoggiaturas in major sevenths, and sometimes with an augmented fifth in a chord of the eleventh. It is this particular and characteristic use of unresolved appoggiaturas that imparts a peculiarly acid flavour to so much of his music, although his sometimes very complex-looking harmonies can usually be analysed and reduced to simpler terms, almost always in relation to conventional harmony with a definitely tonal basis or core.

The final judgment on Ravel must be that while he cannot be considered a seminal influence on developments in modern music in the sense that Debussy undoubtedly was, his will always be one of the great names in twentieth-century French music; and now that the sterile polemics and rivalries of which he was at one time the centre have long been forgotten, he is universally recognised for what he was—a great musician who, in his ceaseless quest for perfection, has enriched our musical heritage with a number of flawless works by which he will always be remembered.

Another contemporary of both Debussy and Ravel who played an important part in the 'liberating' movement in French music during the last years of the nineteenth and first two decades of the twentieth century, was that strange, enigmatic figure Erik Satie, one of the most original and intriguing figures in the whole history of music. Born at Honfleur in Normandy in 1866, he died in Paris, where he had lived throughout his working life, in 1925, and thus lived through one of the most fertile and creative periods in the arts, witnessing the first breath-taking manifestations of Diaghilev's Russian Ballet, the birth of Cubist painting, the innovations of Schoenberg and Stravinsky, and experiencing at the same time the physical and moral dislocations and upheavals of the 1914 war. He also felt the impact of subversive movements like Dada, and Surrealism in its early stages before it developed into a new aesthetic concept which was to have a definite influence on the arts for many years to come.

Erik Alfred Leslie Satie was the eldest of three children born to Alfred Satie, established as a ship's broker in the little port

Vers l'A-zur at-ten-dri d'Oc-to-bre pâle et pur_____ Qui

mire aux grands bassins sa lan-gueur in-fi-nie_____

Un peu plus lent

Un peu plus lent

1ᵉʳ Mouvᵗ

Et lais-se,_____ sur l'eau morte où la

1ᵉʳ Mouvᵗ

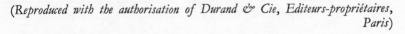

Page from the piano score of Ravel's
'Trois poèmes de Stéphane Mallarmé'

Facsimile of Er.

La Pieuvre

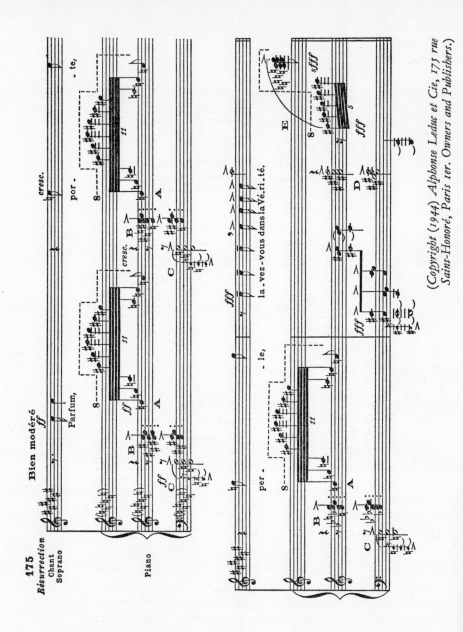

(Copyright (1944) Alphonse Leduc et Cie, 175 rue Saint-Honoré, Paris 1er. Owners and Publishers.)

No. 175 of Messiaen's 'Technique de mon langage musical'

"The volleys in bird style (at A.) contrast with the powerful solemnity of the chords, B. preceded at C. by their effect of inferior resonance. At D., chord of the dominant seventh with added sixth. At E., last volley, like a blow of instantaneous light!"—Translation of composer's note by John Satterfield.

of Honfleur, and his Scottish wife, *née* Jane Leslie Anton. He was thus of mixed Norman and Scottish descent, a fact which may well account for certain of his peculiarities, notably the particular brand of pawky humour for which he was noted (the French call it 'pince-sans-rire'), a trait he had in common with another famous native of Honfleur, the humorist writer Alphonse Allais.

His mother died when he was only six, but it was not long before his father married again—this time a young woman who had been a pupil of the well-known organist Alexandre Guilmant and had theories about the kind of musical education her step-son ought to receive. Unfortunately he took a cordial dislike to her and refused to respond to her efforts to guide his steps in what she considered the right musical paths. Her views were conventional and academic, and already the young Erik was instinctively opposed to them. Nevertheless he was sent when only thirteen to the Paris Conservatoire where he failed to impress any of his teachers, but inevitably acquired that hatred of officialdom in any form, but especially in the arts, which was to remain with him all his life. It seems clear, indeed, that as regards his musical formation, he owed far more to the teaching of the organist at Honfleur, a certain M. Vinot, who gave him his first piano lessons and initiated him into the beauties of Gregorian chant which had such a marked influence on his style in later years. Already this influence can be seen in one of his very earliest compositions, a set of pieces for the piano which appeared in 1886 under the mysterious title of *Ogives*, his intention being apparently to convey a 'Gothic' atmosphere in sound by means of a succession of unrelated common chords moving at a slow, unaccented procession across the bar-less page—a procedure which is characteristic of the music of his 'first period'. But perhaps the most important, historically, of his early works were the three Sarabandes (1887) in which Satie anticipated the harmonic language to be adopted and developed later by Debussy and Ravel (sequences of unresolved chords of the ninth) and the three exquisite

Gymnopédies (1888) in which he foreshadowed the new linear style he was to develop in later years. Small wonder, then, that Debussy (whom Satie first met when he was earning his living playing the piano at the famous Montmartre cabaret *L'Auberge du Clou*) was captivated by the charm and freshness of these little pieces no less than by their complete and absolute originality, running counter to the fashionable Wagnerian aesthetic and the prevalent taste at that time for the grandiose and the flamboyant in modern music—so much so that he took the trouble to orchestrate two of the *Gymnopédies* and conduct them himself.

It was during his Montmartre period, when the young Satie was living in poverty but already showing signs of an extraordinary talent and temperament that he first came in contact with a writer, who was enjoying a certain notoriety at the time, named Joseph Péladan (1859–1918). At the age of twenty-three Péladan had caused something of a sensation in the literary world with his novel *Le Vice Suprême* which ran into twenty editions and carried a preface by Barbey d'Aurévilly, the Right-wing novelist and critic, who had a taste for the extravagant and the bizarre and was the author of novels and stories with such titles as *L'Ensorcelée* and *Les Diaboliques*. Péladan was the Head of the Rosicrucian movement in France, and had appointed himself the High Priest, or 'Sâr' of the 'Rose-Croix du Temple et du Graal' and of an organisation which he called the 'Chaldean Confraternity' the object of which, according to its founder, was to regulate the arts according to what was alleged to be the 'Wagnerian aesthetic'. It would appear that the main influence at work here was that of *Parsifal* which had inspired Péladan to create a Catholic variety of Rosicrucianism in France. His main object as a writer seems to have been to reconcile the Occult, with which he was greatly preoccupied, with orthodox religion, as can be seen from the titles of some of his principal works: *Comment on devient Mage; Comment on devient Fée; L'Occulte Catholique; Le Fils des Etoiles; Le mystère du Graal; La terre du Sphinx* and *La terre du Christ*. In later life Péladan renounced his extravagant claims to be a Seer and High Priest of the Occult, and became outwardly more conventional, but claimed to have taught 'a lesson of beauty and grandeur'.

There is evidence that Satie was already familiar with the writings of Joseph Péladan who, with Flaubert, was one of the authors whose works he had read while convalescing after leaving the army at the end of his period of military service in 1886. And so, when Péladan offered him the post of official composer to the Rose-Croix organisation, Satie was delighted. The chief compositions dating from this period are the incidental music (three Preludes) for Péladan's play *Le Fils des Etoiles* (1891); *Trois sonneries de la Rose-Croix* (1892), and the Prelude to *La porte héroïque du ciel*, an 'esoteric drama' by a colleague of Péladan, Jules Bois. Satie's music of this period was decorative, static, and relied for its effect upon a certain hypnotic quality induced by repetition and the use of harmonies evocative of, if not derived from, Plainsong. It has been suggested by one critic[1] that the reason why Satie was attracted at an early age by the study of Plainsong may have been that 'he saw in the impersonality, aloofness and remoteness from all subjective dramatic stress of this music, qualities which might, with appropriate modifications, approximate to his own uniquely lonely mode of utterance'. This seems highly probable. There was, in any case, nothing 'Wagnerian' about Satie's music; quite the contrary. Yet, though neither Péladan nor anyone else connected with 'Chaldean Confraternity' seems to have noticed any discrepancy between this music and their own theories, they must have felt that, if not particularly 'Wagnerian', it was at least sufficiently 'mystical' and ritualistic to conform to the requirements of the Order, and even attempted to prevent performances of Satie's music elsewhere except by special permission of the High Priest.

Satie, however, had no intention of losing his independence and saw that it was time to break away. He was quite content

[1] W. H. Mellers: *Studies in contemporary music*, London 1948.

to make use of the Rose-Croix to facilitate performances of his works, but objected to being identified in any way with their beliefs and aims, and was certainly not prepared to conform to their aesthetic theories. The end of the collaboration came when he addressed a letter, couched in pseudo-archaic French, to the Editor of the Parisian review *Gil Blas* denying that he was in any sense a 'disciple' of Joseph Péladan, as the latter had suggested, but had been at most his collaborator, and refuting vigorously any suggestion that he had been influenced by the religious or aesthetic theories of the Sâr.

Satie's next move was to found a 'Church' himself, to which he gave the extraordinary title of *L'Eglise Métropolitaine d'Art de Jésus Conducteur*, appointing himself 'Parcier' and 'Maître de chapelle', and at the same time editing a short-lived journal entitled *Le Cartulaire de l'Eglise Métropolitaine d'Art de Jésus Conducteur*. The aim of this fantastic body was 'to fight against those who have neither convictions nor beliefs, no thoughts in their souls nor principles in their hearts', and to protect against 'those responsible for the moral and aesthetic decadence of our time'. The real object of all this seems, however, to have been to provide Satie with a means of publishing violent diatribes against his enemies, and castigating publicly his particular bugbears in the journalistic and artistic world. Already his reputation as an eccentric was established, and he was now ready to embark on the second important phase in his career.

To this period belongs the kind of music with which his name is popularly associated today, characterised by such eccentricities (at that time) as the suppression of time and key signatures and bar-lines, and by the addition of a verbal running commentary superimposed upon the music. Well-known examples of these literary quips—to quote only a few (they are mostly untranslatable)—are: 'Du bout de la pensée', 'Postulez en vous-même', 'Sur la langue', 'Ouvrez la tête', etc., while to the pieces themselves he gave such strange titles as: *Embryons désséchés, Croquis et agaceries d'un gros bonhomme en bois,*

Danses de travers and *Avant-dernières pensées*. It should be
stressed, however, that in nearly all these pieces the music
itself is completely serious and straightforward, and should be
listened to as such. Jean Cocteau's theory that Satie gave comic
titles to his music 'in order to protect his works from persons
obsessed with the sublime' is probably correct; it may also
have been his way of poking fun at the somewhat 'precious'
titles favoured by Debussy and the Impressionists. The greatest
mistake is to believe that because of the title the music itself
must be trivial. With Satie, this is never so. He was the first
composer to re-think music, and to write music about music.
Though he worked habitually on a small scale, he saw very
clearly. The American composer and critic Virgil Thomson
claims that Satie: 'invented the only twentieth-century musical
aesthetic in the Western world—quietude, precision, acuteness
of auditory observation, gentleness, sincerity and directness of
statement'; and, speaking of the piano works with the
humorous titles, he puts them in their right perspective in the
following profoundly perceptive words: 'To the uninitiated
these pieces sound trifling. To those who love them they are
fresh and beautiful and firmly right. . . . And that freshness and
rightness have long dominated the musical thought of France.
Any attempt to penetrate that musical thought without first
penetrating that of Satie is fruitless.'

That Satie was not only a miniaturist, however, is shown by
the fact that he wrote at least two major works—the revolutionary ballet *Parade* produced in 1917 in collaboration with
Cocteau and Picasso and Diaghilev's Russian Ballet—a work
which to this day is a landmark in the history of the theatre—
and *Socrate*, a musical setting of selected passages from the
Dialogues of Plato, a work of quiet and meditative beauty which
disposes once and for all of any misguided suggestions that Satie
has no real claim to be considered a 'serious' musician. With
the passage of time, on the contrary, his importance as a seminal force in the evolution of modern music is becoming more
and more generally recognised; and it can now be seen that

Georges Auric was right many years ago when he remarked that Satie's works, 'although written without reference to the prevailing taste and style of the day, have in reality *anticipated* those tastes and styles with the most astonishing precision'. Satie, in fact, gave expression to what was *latent* in the consciousness of the world in which he lived; and it is this that makes him seem to belong so unmistakably to our epoch in his ideas and general approach to music. Thus, in the Sarabandes, for example (composed in 1887), he foreshadowed the lines on which modern harmony was going to be developed by Debussy and other twentieth-century composers; the nostalgic *Gymnopédies*, written at the same period but entirely without reference to any contemporary model, point the way to that return to the old French traditions and a generally modal style which was exemplified later in the works of Debussy and Ravel; and then, in the heyday of Impressionism about 1912, came the *Préludes flasques* which, in their linear austerity, heralded the neoclassic vogue which was to dominate Western music during the nineteen-twenties. Then again, *Parade* (1917) was certainly the precursor of a good deal of the 'mechanistic' music which was a feature of the post-first world war years (and, indeed, still much in evidence today) while the *Piège de Méduse*, composed in 1913 anticipated Dada by some three years just as surely as the *Heures séculaires et instantanées* of 1914, and especially the texts that accompanied them, can now be seen to be of purely Surrealist inspiration before even the term had been invented.

And so it was perhaps inevitable that many years later, in the last year of his life, he was called upon to write the music for a ballet that really was surrealist. This was *Relâche*, with scenario and scenery by the avant-garde artists Francis Picabia and Marcel Duchamp, with a hilarious *Entr'acte cinématographique* by René Clair for which Satie not only composed the music, but appeared in himself. In one sequence he was seen firing a cannon on the roof of the Théâtre des Champs-Elysées, and clambering over the gargoyles on Notre Dame.

The ballet itself was fantastic and grotesque, but characteristic-ally, the music he wrote to accompany it was dry and rather formal, mainly consisting of conventional *entrées* and classical dance movements, with here and there a popular tune that the public was delighted to recognise. *Relâche* had a sensational *succès de scandale*, but added little to Satie's reputation as a serious musician, and estranged him from some of his old friends who thought this time he had gone too far. It must be looked upon as a last defiant gesture of sympathy and soli-darity with the avant-garde; and although it is by other works of a rarer and more enduring quality that Erik Satie will always be remembered, it is in keeping with the enigmatic, dual personality of this fundamentally wise and dedicated musician that he should have chosen to make his exit wearing his jester's mask.

It is, then, this duality, this versatility, this prophetic aware-ness of where current trends were leading (did he not say: 'L'avenir me donnera raison. N'ai-je pas été déjà bon pro-phète?') *plus* the fact that, so far from being 'with' any move-ment, however avant-garde, he was usually at least one, if not two steps ahead, that makes Satie seem today, in a very real sense, a 'contemporary' composer, belonging to today as much as to yesterday. Moreover, it is probable that in fifty, or even a hundred years from now—always assuming that by then he will not have been forgotten altogether—his music will still seem 'modern' in a certain sense, in so far as it has a curious timeless, or rather dateless quality about it which makes it seem not to belong to any particular period, but at the same time to be prophetic—looking forward rather than back. Satie, as we have seen, may have had his own good reasons for adopting, when it suited him, a comic disguise—a procedure fraught with certain dangers, for often the disguise did its work only too well, and the mask was mistaken for the man. Yet if we succeed in getting behind that mask, we shall find underneath the figure of an immensely sincere, courageous and profoundly original artist. The significance of Satie lies in the

isolation into which he deliberately withdrew in order to pursue
to the end the ideals which seemed to him important; and it is
this disregard of contemporary fashions, this concentration on
certain aspects of the art of music which no one else has ever
bothered about, this ploughing of a lonely furrow that makes
Satie's contribution to Western art unique.

One of the most endearing features of Satie's complex nature
was the sympathy he always felt for, and the encouragement he
gave to young musicians; he was always the champion of
youth and of new movements, and felt that music would be
safe in their hands. 'La jeunesse présente et future', he wrote
two years before he died, 'se chargera de mettre les choses au
point.' This was the miracle referred to by Milhaud (a former
disciple and lifelong admirer) by virtue of which 'Satie remains eternally the youngest of the young, while his works invariably satisfied the aspiration of the latest comers. He knew
well that a younger generation would always stand up for him
and love him for the perfection of his music and for his complete and uncompromising sincerity.'

Thus it was that after the 'scandal' of *Parade* in 1917 (for the
ballet was far too 'advanced' for the Parisian war-time public
and had a very hostile reception) Satie had the satisfaction of
soon finding himself at the head of a new 'movement' in
which he was to play the role of Mentor to a group of young
musicians who sensed in the composer of *Parade* a new force in
music and the incarnation of 'l'esprit nouveau'—that spirit of
rejuvenation of which they felt their art was so badly in need.
The young musicians who rallied round Satie at this time were
later to become famous as 'Les Six'; but before they were thus
designated, Satie had dubbed them 'Les Nouveaux Jeunes'. It
was not in fact until 1921, as the result of an article published
in *Comœdia* by the critic Henri Collet under the title '*Les cinq
Russes, les six Français et Erik Satie*' that the group name of 'Les
Six' was first applied to six young musicians, united as much
by friendship as by any tastes they may have had in common,
whose names were Darius Milhaud, Louis Durey, Georges

Auric, Arthur Honegger, Francis Poulenc and Germaine Tailleferre. Honegger and Milhaud had been pupils of the famous teacher Gédalge at the Paris Conservatoire; Auric, who came to Paris from Montpellier, had studied with Vincent d'Indy at the Schola before going to the Conservatoire; Durey, the eldest of the group, had also studied at the Schola and Tailleferre at the Conservatoire; while Poulenc had been a pupil of Koechlin for harmony and of Ricardo Viñes, who was to be closely associated with the group, for piano. The group's first concerts were given at the theatre *Le Vieux Colombier* in 1918, under Satie's supervision, and the new unfamiliar music of these young people, with its 'wrong note' harmonies, crude dissonances and carefully cultivated irreverence, scandalised their audiences at first, whose reactions were duly recorded in the press thus ensuring for the group the publicity which helped to launch them on their respective careers. For it soon became apparent that the differences between them individually were at least as great as the community of views and mutual sympathy which united them as friends. In retrospect the real significance of 'Les Six' as a group is that they, following Satie's example, were the first to kick over the traces, as it were, of the conventions and traditions to which 'serious' music in France, despite the innovations of pioneers like Debussy and Ravel, had always more or less conformed, thus preparing the way for the break-through that ushered in the new developments in music that can be said to date from world war I. Schoenberg and Stravinsky in their different ways (*Pierrot Lunaire* in 1912, *The Rite of Spring* in 1913) were already speaking a new language; but the Six were the first, since the death of Debussy, to do anything at all comparable in France. What they all had in common was a conviction that it was time to react against what they considered to be the unhealthy over-refinement and sophistication of the pre-war school of which Debussy and Ravel were the most eminent representatives. They objected to what they called Ravel's *'écriture artiste'* and Debussy's alleged 'Impressionism', taking their lead from

Jean Cocteau who wrote his brilliant little pamphlet *Le Coq et l'Arlequin* to commend to them the example of Erik Satie and to give them an aesthetic and theoretic platform from which to launch their offensive. According to Cocteau (in 1919): 'Debussy missed his way because he fell from the German frying-pan into the Russian fire. Once again the pedal blurs rhythm and creates a fluid atmosphere congenial to *short-sighted ears*. Satie remains intact. Hear his *Gymnopédies*, so clear in their form and melancholy feeling. Debussy orchestrates them, confuses them and wraps their exquisite architecture in a cloud. . . . Satie speaks of Ingres: Debussy transposes Claude Monet "à la Russe". Enough of hammocks, garlands and gondolas; I want someone to build me music I can live in like a house.' There is, of course, a grain of truth in all this (though Cocteau in later life freely acknowledged Debussy's greatness) but the young musicians took it as their gospel. And so began the cult of homely melodies, crude, square-cut rhythms and a musical atmosphere redolent of circus sawdust and village bands, tempered with a dash of jazz to give it a more exotic flavour, and a lavish use of polytonal discords. To this period belong such works as Milhaud's *Le bœuf sur le toit*, Cocteau's scenic fantasy *Les Mariés de la Tour Eiffel* for which all the Six (except Durey) wrote music, and Poulenc's setting of Cocteau's *Cocardes* in which he scored the accompaniment for violin, cornet, trombone, bass drum and triangle, thus imitating very successfully the sounds produced by a street-corner band. Auric's fox-trot, *Adieu New York*, and Milhaud's settings to music of catalogues of flowers and agricultural instruments are also typical of this period.

After these first youthful extravagances, however (which reflected admittedly, a certain desire for publicity and a mischievous urge to *épater le bourgeois*), it soon became clear that each member of the group was a distinct personality with a style of his own, and in a few years' time they had begun to drift (musically speaking) apart.[1]

[1] This fact did not escape Cocteau's notice, and he recognised in the

Darius Milhaud (b. 1892), who came from an old Jewish-Provençal family and was born in Aix-en-Provence, developed his own very personal style at an early age and has been one of the most prolific of twentieth-century French composers with a catalogue of well over 400 opus numbers to his credit comprising eight operas, ten ballets, numerous choral works, a quantity of film and theatre music, eighteen string quartets, fourteen concertos, eight symphonies and a mass of vocal and piano music to mention only a few items in his vast output. There is a vein of harshness that runs through all his work, but his music, if completely a-sensuous and devoid of frills, has immense vitality and a kind of streamlined dynamism that is the hallmark of his very characteristic style. And as in Milhaud's case the difference in style between his latest and his earliest works is, by and large, less noticeable than in the case of the majority of his contemporaries, some of his best early works, such as the ballets *L'Homme et son désir* and *La Création du monde* (1921 and 1923), the *Poèmes juifs* (1916) or the *Saudades do Brasil* (1921) can give as good an idea of the essential Milhaud as any of his later and perhaps quantitatively more important works, many of which were written in the U.S.A. where much

---

following verses, not without some undertones of regret, that the ties which had united the little band he had so carefully nursed were loosening, if not already severed:

> Auric, Milhaud, Poulenc, Tailleferre, Honegger
> J'a mis votre bouquet dans l'eau du même vase,
> Et vous ai chèrement tortillé par la base
> Tous libres de choisir votre chemin en l'air.
>
> Or chacun étoilant d'autres feux sa fusée,
> Qui laisse choir ailleurs son musical arceau,
> Me sera quelque jour la gloire refusée
> D'être le gardien nocturne du faisceau.
>
> Je n'imite la rose et sa dure lancette,
> Aspirant goulûment le sang du rossignol,
> Et montre de mon cœur la profonde recette
> Pour que ces amis-là puissent prendre leur vol.

of his time has been spent since the 1939 war as director of music at Mill's College, in California.

Georges Auric (b. 1899) made his début as a serious composer under the aegis of Diaghilev for whose Russian Ballet he wrote three ballets: *Les Fâcheux* (after Molière) in 1923, *Les Matelots* and *La Pastorale* in 1925–6. Subsequently he became widely known for the film-music he wrote for both French and English films, notably René Clair's *A nous la liberté* and Cocteau's *L'Heureux retour* and *L'Aigle à deux têtes*; and in England among others for Shaw's *Caesar and Cleopatra*, *Passport to Pimlico* and *Moulin Rouge*, the music for which became a best-seller. Literary and administrative work has since absorbed much of his time, and he was for many years Director of the Paris Opéra.

Francis Poulenc (1899–1963) excelled above all as a songwriter, as a composer of serious religious music and numerous choral works both sacred and profane, and as a pianist who wrote for his instrument a number of delightful works. He had the gift of spontaneous melodic invention and an easy charm and fluency that make his music immediately appealing; and in his dual personality there was room for both frivolity, wit and sophistication and for a deeply thoughtful and serious attitude towards life which is reflected in his religious music (he was a devout though far from bigoted Catholic) in which he often attained, by the simplest means, heights of genuine, though never over-dramatised, religious fervour. Among his finest works in this vein are the *Litanies à la Vierge Noire de Rocamadour*, the four Motets, the Mass, the Stabat Mater and the remarkable *Sept Répons des Ténèbres* which was almost his last work. During the 1939–45 war Poulenc played a prominent part in the 'musical resistance' movement, and one of the most impressive of his choral works was the cantata for double chorus *a cappella*, *Figure Humaine*, composed during the German occupation of France (1940–5) on poems by Paul Eluard, including an impassioned hymn to Liberty, of which the B.B.C. gave the first performance anywhere in 1945. His

two operas, *Dialogues des Carmélites* and *La Voix humaine*, one
of his last works, were also produced with success in Europe
and America shortly before he died.

Like Milhaud and Auric, and other composers of his generation, Poulenc also came under the spell of Diaghilev who commissioned him to write a ballet. This was *Les Biches* which, with
décors and costumes by Marie Laurencin, was produced in
Monte Carlo in 1923 and was an instant success. In the Ragtime
scene Poulence showed his mastery of the jazz idiom of the
period, while in the delicate Adagietto he struck a note of
romantic lyricism that from then on was to become one of the
main characteristics of his later music. Almost alone among
his contemporaries he wrote music unashamedly to give
pleasure, and though keenly aware of all the trends and
currents of contemporary musical fashions, his only desire
was to express in music, whether grave or gay, whatever his
heart dictated.

With Arthur Honegger (1892–1955), whose inclusion in the
group of Six was almost a matter of chance, we enter a different
world. Never really in sympathy with the much publicised
aims and theories of the group in which he found himself, his
tastes and musical formation had always been mainly classical,
as is evident in most of his mature works. Even in the biblical
drama for chorus and orchestra, *Le Roi David*, with which he
made his name in 1921, there is an element of solid craftsmanship and serious purpose which is lacking in the earliest works
of most of his contemporaries; and though the idiom is force-
ful enough, and much of the music aggressively polytonal
according to the fashion of the day, the work has a kind of
classical consistency and sincerity that gives it real distinction.
The best of Honegger is probably to be found in certain other
early works, such as the 'mimed symphony' *Horace Victorieux*
(1921), *Pacific 231* (1923), a realistic impression of a locomotive
gathering speed, and the incidental music he wrote for
Cocteau's *Antigone*; while among the later works notable
examples of his mature style are the dramatic oratorios *Amphion*

and *Jeanne d'Arc au bûcher*. Between 1930 and 1951 he wrote five symphonies, of which perhaps the best known are the third, the *Symphonie liturgique* and the fifth, sub-titled 'di tre re' composed in 1951. Honegger's output was considerable, and covers a wide field, comprising a number of stage works, ballets and incidental music, music for films, songs and a number of choral and orchestral works as well as chamber music. He was a composer of real substance whose work since his death has tended, somewhat unjustly, to be overlooked.

Germaine Tailleferre (b. 1892), as the only woman member of the 'Six', attracted immediate attention with her early compositions which were remarkable for their youthful freshness and vitality, but she was productive only up to the 1939 war and the time of her marriage, since when she has lived in the United States. Her Violin and Piano Sonata (1922) was given its first performance by Jacques Thibaut and Alfred Cortot; and among other works of this period the most important were *Jeux de plein air* for two pianos, the *Ballade* for piano and orchestra and the ballet *Le marchand des oiseaux* produced by the Swedish Ballet of Jean Borlin in 1923. Her Piano Concertino in D was in Cortot's repertory, and was heard in London under the direction of Sir Henry Wood. Her last work to be produced in France was the *opéra-bouffe Le Marin du Bolivar* specially composed for the Paris Exhibition of 1937.

Louis Durey (b. 1888) seceded from the Group as early as 1921, and has since lived in seclusion in the south of France. His early works showed great promise and accomplishment, notably his *Images à Crusoë*, a song-cycle with instrumental accompaniment on poems by Saint-Léger, two string quartets, a string trio and *Le Bestiaire*, another song-cycle consisting of settings of miniature poems descriptive of animals by Guillaume Apollinaire. Whether the quality of his early work has been maintained since he left the Group is difficult to say as, although he was still writing music at the age of 82, very little of his later work has been published. His political views caused him to adhere to the so-called 'Progressist' movement sponsored at one time by iron-curtain countries desirous of providing 'music for the masses', and this factor, combined with his interest in folk-music, has no doubt tended to colour all his later output.

After the Six had been successfully launched, Satie turned his attention to yet another group of young musicians who had been recommended to him by Darius Milhaud and came to be known as the 'Ecole d'Arcueil', taking their name from the Parisian suburb where the 'Bon Maître' lived. Satie took the unusual step of introducing them to the public at a concert he organised at the Collège de France: their names were Roger Désormière, Henri Cliquet-Pleyel, Maxime Jacob and Henri Sauguet. Désormière made his name subsequently as a conductor, but both he and Cliquet-Pleyel died prematurely; Maxime Jacob is now a Benedictine monk, but still composing, while Sauguet (see Chapter 8) is now, with Milhaud, one of the doyens of contemporary French music.

The real significance of the Cocteau-Satie-Les Six aesthetic and intellectual crusade to bring about a renovation of French music after the first world war can only now, perhaps, be seen in its true perspective. The publicity by which it was surrounded at the time, and the polemics and partisan passions to which it gave rise, tended to obscure and distort its fundamentally sound and simple aims. The war, during which all lines of communication with the past had, in a sense, been cut, had created a kind of intellectual and artistic vacuum, and all the old values were in the melting-pot. The same thing happened after the second world war, only this time the young composers, for some mysterious reason, looked backwards and wrote their 'new music' in accordance with the teaching of the Viennese school, Schoenberg, Berg and Webern, who had enjoyed a certain vogue in the nineteen-twenties and were now being re-discovered by the avant-garde of the nineteen-forties and fifties. But the musical climate in which the Six grew up was very different. Milhaud was only twenty-one and most of the others in their teens when Stravinsky's *Rite of Spring*

exploded like a bomb, apparently destroying music's last lines of
communication with her traditional past. At the same time, at
the opposite end of the spectrum as it were, another new voice
was making itself heard—the still, quiet voice of Erik Satie
who, since 1887, had been unobtrusively organising a modest
revolution of his own. At a time when Wagner was fashionable, Satie was writing his Sarabandes and *Gymnopédies* and
talking to Debussy about the need in France for a music 'sans
choucroute', following rather in the steps of the Impressionist
painters imbued with the clear luminosity of the Ile de France.
Cocteau did not meet Satie until 1915, but he knew his work
and realised his potential importance as the creator of another
kind of 'new music', very different from that of Stravinsky;
and it was this that led him to proclaim (in *Le Coq et l'Arlequin*)
that 'the profound originality of a Satie provides young musicians with a teaching that does not imply the desertion of their
own originality. Wagner, Stravinsky, and even Debussy are
first-rate octopuses. Whoever goes near them is sore put to it
to escape from their tentacles: Satie leaves a clear road open
upon which everyone is free to leave his own imprint.' It
should be noted that this was written in 1918, by which time it
would seem that Cocteau was beginning to have second
thoughts about Stravinsky, although he had, like everyone
else, been greatly impressed by the *Rite of Spring*—a work of
which he said that it 'opened and closed an epoch'. 'We were
then', he said, 'musically in the heyday of Impressionism.
Everyone was trying to find new ways of being vague and in-
distinct. . . . Then, suddenly, in the midst of these charming
ruins there sprang up the Stravinsky tree. When all is said and
done, the *Sacre* is still a 'Fauvist' work, an organised 'Fauvist'
work. Gauguin and Matisse pay homage to it. But if the back-
wardness of music as compared to painting prevented the
Sacre, of necessity, from coinciding exactly with other disturbing elements, it none the less contributed an indispensable
dynamitic force. . . . In brief, the work as it stands was, and is,
a masterpiece; a symphony impregnated with a wild sadness of

primitive earth, camp and farmyard noises, fragments of melodies emerging from the depths of time, animal pantings, profound upheavals, the Georgics of a prehistoric age.'

It is probable that one of the reasons for Cocteau's subsequent change of attitude towards Stravinsky (only temporary, but enough to cause an equally temporary estrangement between them) was a suspicion that through his association with the 'fashionable' Russian Ballet and Diaghilev he was in danger of being spoiled. 'The theatre corrupts everything', he wrote, 'even a Stravinsky . . . I consider the *Sacre du Printemps* a masterpiece, but I discern in the atmosphere created by its production a religious complicity existing among the initiated, like the hypnotism of Bayreuth. Wagner wanted the theatre; Stravinsky finds himself involved in it by circumstances. There is a difference. But even though he composes *in spite of* the theatre, the theatre has none the less infected him with its microbes. Stravinsky gets at us by other means than Wagner; he does not try to hypnotise us or plunge us in semi-darkness; he hits us deliberately over the head and in the heart. . . . Wagner cooks us slowly; Stravinsky does not give us time to say "Ouf!" but both of them upset our nerves. This is music that comes from the bowels; an octopus from which you must flee or else it will devour you. It is the fault of the theatre. . . . Stravinsky will get a man out of a quicksand, but still does not belong to the race of architects. His work is not based on scaffolding—it grows.' (Here it should be noted that Cocteau in a later edition added a footnote saying: 'This unjust remark is, of course, annulled by *l'Histoire du soldat* with which I was then unacquainted, as well as by all Stravinsky's later works.')

All this makes it clear why, feeling as he did at the time, Cocteau in one of his frequent reversals of attitude, felt a craving for the simplicity and clarity which he discerned in Satie, whom he then held up as a model for the young musicians who would, he hoped, turn their backs on Impressionism ('Enough of clouds, waves, aquariums, water-sprites and nocturnal scents; what we need is a music of the earth, everyday music...

music one can live in like a house'); keep clear of the theatre
('The café-concert is often pure; the theatre is always corrupt');
and write the kind of music he dreamed of ('The music I want
must be French, of France.') Finally, as if in echo of what Satie
had said to Debussy in 1891: 'Why shouldn't we use the
methods of Claude Monet, Cézanne, Toulouse-Lautrec, etc.
Nothing simpler; aren't they just expressions?' Cocteau issues
a similar challenge: 'For the last ten years Chardin, Ingres,
Manet and Cézanne have dominated European painting, and
the foreigner comes to us to put his racial gifts to school with
them. Now I declare that French music is going to influence
the world.'

When we reflect that at the time Cocteau was writing this
Ravel, Roussel, Dukas and Koechlin, not to mention veterans
like Fauré, d'Indy and Saint-Saëns, were all alive and still composing, while Debussy's recent death had just come as a re-
minder to the world of music of what it owed to France, it
may seem strange that a Frenchman should have found it
necessary to make this declaration implying that up to now the
influence of French music had been negligible. It must not be
forgotten, however, that the 1914 war came at a time when all
sorts of new ideas and movements affecting the arts were in the
air. Marinetti's Futurism (see Chapter 2) attacking all accepted
values had had a certain subversive effect before it fizzled out;
the new Viennese music (Schoenberg, Berg and Webern) was
encountering opposition everywhere, and a concert in Vienna
in 1912 ended in a riot which had to be quelled by the police;
in painting, there had been the 'Fauves' or 'Post-Impres-
sionists' whose 'modernism' had at one time been found
shocking; but their revolution was nothing in comparison with
that of the so-called 'Cubists' who succeeded them. The term
originated in Cézanne's dictum that everything in Nature was
derived from 'spheres, cones and cylinders'; but it was not
officially adopted until the day when, in rejecting some pictures
designed on these lines which Braque had submitted to the
Salon d'Automne in 1908, Matisse, who was on the jury, de-

scribed them as 'entirely constructed in little cubes'—a remark which led the critic to whom it was made to apply to these same pictures, when exhibited elsewhere, the term 'Cubiste'.[1]

The great champion of Cubism (as, indeed, of all *avant-garde* movements in the arts) was the poet Guillaume Apollinaire (1880–1918) in whose versatile genius every facet of the kaleidoscopic transformations which all the arts were undergoing at that time seemed to be reflected. With prophetic clarity he discerned the shape of things to come, and was one of the first to notice that in *Parade* Cocteau, Picasso and Satie had achieved . . . 'a sort of surrealism in which I see the point of departure for a series of manifestations of that New Spirit which promises to modify the arts and the conduct of life (*mœurs*) from top to bottom in a universal joyousness'.[2]

We have seen how all new movements in the other arts in France invariably have their literary counterpart, and cubism was no exception. It was not long before writers were imitating the deformation of the painters, renouncing (e.g. the Simultanists, see Chapter 2) logic, coherence and reason, and making a cult of the irrational and the unconscious. This was the period, too, when the vogue for primitive negro art was launched after Picasso's discovery of an ebony statuette he had seen in Matisse's studio—an event which inevitably had repercussions in the world of music where jazz rhythms were now admitted in 'serious' scores by any composer wishing to be considered *à la page*. (Notable examples are to be found in Milhaud's *La Création du monde*, Ravel's *Violin Sonata* and *Concerto for the Left Hand*, and Debussy's *Golliwog's Cakewalk* and *Boîte à joujoux*.)

And so it is against this kind of background that the 'Six' made their début; and here, once again, their close affiliations

---

[1] For a full account of the origins of cubism, see R. H. Wilenski: *Modern French Painting*, London 1940.

[2] To have coined the word 'surrealism' some years before the official consecration of what it denotes is typical of Apollinaire's artistic clairvoyance.

with the best writers of the day, and the extent to which they were influenced by contemporary literature, is a point to be noted before we move on to consider other developments on the musical front in the post-first-world-war years. Their favourite authors appear to have been Paul Claudel (the fanatically Catholic poet and dramatist with whom Milhaud especially was closely associated after working with him when he was French ambassador to Brazil during the 1914 war); Valéry, Apollinaire, Eluard, Aragon and, of course, Cocteau. Poulenc alone set more than thirty of Apollinaire's poems as well as his opera-bouffe *Les mamelles de Tirésias*; Claudel was Milhaud's librettist in several of his major stage-works (*Christophe Colomb*, *Les Choéphores*, *L'homme et son désir*) and in countless songs and choral works, and also collaborated with Honegger in *Jeanne d'Arc au bûcher* and *Le soulier de satin*; while Cocteau, besides providing Honegger with the libretto of his opera *Antigone* and Milhaud with the text of his miniature opera *Le pauvre matelot* and the scenarios of *Le Bœuf sur le toit* and *Le train bleu*, was frequently set by all the Six who found in his elegant and allusive verse a challenge to their ingenuity. But perhaps the work which epitomises most successfully the frivolity, inconsequentiality and provocative, if childish, desire to *épater le bourgeois* which characterised 'Les Six' in their early days, was Cocteau's extraordinary (and already surrealist) text for *Les Mariés de la Tour Eiffel* (1921) for which all the Six (except Durey) wrote hilarious music. Here, if anywhere, can be found an example of what Apollinaire foresaw when he spoke of the New Spirit which was going to bring a 'universal joyousness' into life; and to students of the period the work is an invaluable 'source'.[1]

There is another aspect of this situation in which, as we have seen, these young musicians were not only aware of, but to some extent influenced by whatever was new or significant in the literature of their day, and that is that the men of letters

[1] Fortunately it has been reconstituted and is now available on disk: ADES 15501.

tended to show an equal interest in the latest developments in music. The situation in fact had changed little since the days of the Symbolists and the Parnassians (see Chapter 5), only now instead of Mallarmé, Baudelaire, Henri de Régnier and Villiers de l'Isle-Adam for example, the musically-minded writers were Claudel, Gide, Valéry, Jacques Rivière (in his published *Correspondance* with Alain Fournier and his chronicles in the *Nouvelle Revue Française* prior to the 1914 war), Proust and Cocteau. Apollinaire, though disclaiming any knowledge of music ('La musique à laquelle pour ma part je ne connais rien'), must be mentioned in this connexion if only because of the strangely musical quality of much of his verse (he always sang as he composed his poems) which was one of the reasons no doubt, why so many composers wanted to set his work to music. Moreover the fact that he recognised the originality of composers like Varèse and Satie, though perhaps for not exclusively musical reasons, shows that he was at least aware of current trends in music, though he was, of course, far more interested in the plastic arts. It is also not without significance that when he coined the word 'Orphism' to describe the harmonies of pure colour he discerned in the first abstract paintings of Robert Delaunay (who said himself that he 'played with colours as if they were musical phrases in a fugue . . .'), he was applying to painting a term with definite musical associations.

With writers like Claudel and Gide, however, we are on very different ground. Gide was an amateur pianist who wrote a book on Chopin, while Claudel wrote abundantly about music and personally supervised, down to the smallest details, the work of any musician engaged on setting his texts to music. Both Milhaud and Honegger have described how the poet would show them exactly what kind of music he wanted at any given point in his text—where it should be melody and where spoken recitative, for example; and when Honegger was composing, on a poem by Claudel, his choral work *La danse des morts* the poet, he tells us, indicated details of scoring and even, in one realistic passage entitled *Sanglots*, 'actually dictated these sobs to me—the hollow cry of despair, the convulsive sighs and the final choking intake of breath . . .'. Claudel was at one time, like so many men of letters, a fervent admirer of Wagner; but later in life—again like so many of his contemporaries— he turned against him, attacking him savagely (and largely for the wrong reasons) in his notorious *Le poison Wagnérien*.

The case of Marcel Proust is rather different, his attitude towards music being largely that of a dilettante, although the allusions to and discussions about music in his great work *A la recherche du temps perdu* are so numerous and, in a sense, important, that they have been the subject of many articles and books.

Attempts have even been made to show that *A la recherche* is constructed in accordance with the principles of musical composition, and is, as it were, a kind of vast literary symphony. This would be difficult to sustain (though the analogy has a certain superficial plausibility) since we know that Proust had no technical knowledge of music which, for him, was essentially a medium for purely sensuous and emotional impressions providing, as it were, a kind of atmospheric background for certain specific states of mind. His approach was, in fact, entirely subjective; he appreciated music for the effect it had on him, and was not concerned with any other aspect; nor would he have been capable of judging objectively the merits or demerits of any particular work on purely musical grounds. Nevertheless his tastes, if unadventurous, were irreproachable as far as they went, and in line with those of the majority of late nineteenth-century musically-minded French writers for whom, in the words of Jules Janin, famous dramatic critic of the *Journal des Débats*, 'La musique, c'est l'art nouveau de la France, c'est notre passion nouvelle.' And it was precisely these writers—notably Stendhal, George Sand, Gérard de Nerval, Baudelaire, de Vigny, Villiers de l'Isle-Adam, Catulle Mendès and above all Mallarmé—that Proust valued most highly and referred to most frequently, sharing their admiration for Chopin, Schumann and Liszt and, of course, Wagner. He was also an admirer of César Franck and, among the 'moderns', Fauré and, to some extent and more adventurously, Debussy. Here, he must have felt, was a new and authentically French voice and a rare sensibility not unlike his own. The attraction he felt for this music may also have been slightly coloured by a desire to be *à la page*; for Proust was not exempt from a certain artistic, as well as social *snobisme* which may also have accounted for his often declared, but somehow slightly improbable admiration for the late quartets of Beethoven. At all events, there are several references to *Pelléas* in *A la recherche*, notably to the scene where Pelléas, emerging from the grotto by the sea, exclaims: 'Ah! je respire enfin'— scene which Proust compares to the liberation of the prisoners in *Fidelio*, and also associates with the scent of roses. There is, moreover, a curious episode in the novel,[1] showing that Proust's familiarity with *Pelléas* was more than superficial, where he compares the street-cries he heard from the window of his padded room to certain recitatifs in Mussorgsky's *Boris Godunov*, and also to one of the old King Arkel's utterances in *Pelléas*. In this instance it was the way in which an itinerant seller of snails, after pronouncing the words: 'Les escargots, ils sont frais, ils sont beaux' in an ordinary speaking voice, added in a kind of melodic chant: 'On les vend six sous la douzaine', that reminded Proust so vividly of a scene in *Pelléas*. 'I have never been able to understand', he writes, 'why these simple words were uttered in such an inappropriate tone of voice, as mysterious as the secret that causes everyone to be so sad in the old palace where Mélisande failed to bring joy, and as profound as the thoughts of the old King Arkel who tries, in simple words, to sum up all wisdom and mortal destiny. The very notes in which the voice of the old king of Allemonde pronounces, with increasing tenderness, the words:

[1] The incident is quoted in George Piroué's *Proust et la musique du devenir*, Paris 1960, and occurs in *A la recherche du temps perdu*, Vol. III, pp. 117–18.

"It may seem strange, but perhaps there is a reason for everything that happens . . .", or again: "There is no reason to be
afraid; she was a poor mysterious little being, like everyone
else . . ." were the same as those used by the snail-seller repeating indefinitely the words: "On les vend six sous la douzaine."
. . .'

The passage shows that Proust must have had a perceptive
ear, and a sensitivity of the same order as that of Debussy himself. Although it is on record that the two men used sometimes
to meet at the Taverne Weber in the rue Royale, and that on
one occasion Proust invited Debussy to one of his famous
parties (an invitation that was declined), it seems clear that beneath the surface they had little in common and moved in very
different spheres.

No discussion of music in the work of Proust would be
complete without some reference to the famous 'petite phrase'
in the sonata by Proust's imaginary composer Vinteuil. It has
now been established that the 'petite phrase' itself occurs in
the Saint-Saëns violin sonata in D minor (as Proust confessed
in a letter to his friend Jacques de Lacretelle, although Saint-
Saëns was not a composer he admired), but that both in the
sonata and the septet the author, in his description of the effect
the music had upon various listeners, probably also had in
mind certain passages from such widely different composers
as Fauré, Franck and Debussy.

There are also frequent references to Wagner, especially to
Parsifal (Good Friday music), *Lohengrin*, *Tannhaüser* and *Tristan*;
but it may well be that Proust's obsession with Wagner arose
from a feeling that there was a certain bond between them in
that, just as Wagner had been one of the first to introduce
literature into music, so had he himself been a pioneer in introducing music into literature. At all events, though we may
still feel that Proust was devoted to music for reasons not
strictly musical, we have it on his own confession that, as he
told one of his biographers Benoist-Méchin: 'Music has been
one of the greatest passions in my life. I say *has been*, because

now I have scarcely any opportunity of hearing any except in my memories. It has brought me ineffable joys and certitudes— the proof that there exists something other than the void I have encountered on all sides; it runs like a guide-line throughout all my work.'

Thus it is possible to see in Marcel Proust the final apotheosis, as it were, of that *rapprochement* between music and letters that had been, as we have seen, so marked a feature of the artistic climate in late nineteenth- and early twentieth-century France, and was still in evidence when the curtain rose on the next scene in our review of events between the wars, ushering in the nineteen-thirties.

CHAPTER EIGHT

The nineteen-thirties;
Varèse, Jolivet and the 'Independents'

The years that immediately preceded world war II—that is to say the early nineteen-thirties—have sometimes been referred to as the period of musical 'humanism' in contrast to the anti-romantic, anti-expressionist, objective, down-to-earth attitude of the 'twenties. In the reaction against emotionalism of any kind—against, as Cocteau put it, the kind of music 'one listens to with one's head in one's hands' (e.g. Wagner and Debussy) —simplification became the order of the day. Music must be purged of feeling and emotion of any kind, and become a limpid stream, a passionless pattern of abstract sounds, a *parterre* of arabesques, objective, inhuman and precise. 'Back to Bach' was the slogan of the neo-classicists, or at any rate, back to the eighteenth century, when music wore ruffles and a wig and was content to express nothing but itself. Stravinsky himself was largely responsible for the neo-classicism which held sway during the nineteen-twenties, contributing in that vein such works as the Piano Concerto (1924), the Sonata and Serenade for piano (1922–5), the Octuor (1923) and the ballet *Apollon Musagète* (1927). His example was followed by a host of imitators, and quantities of colourless works were presented, in monotonous succession, at festivals of the International Society for Contemporary Music—the production of a mistaken theory according to which music had to be puerile in order to be pure.

This idealisation of the seventeenth and eighteenth centuries was also based on a misunderstanding of their true nature, since every other characteristic of the music of the period except its texture and style, was ignored. The result was a plethora of *pastiches* of Scarlatti, Haydn and Bach which lacked all the qualities which distinguish these composers from the rabble of their contemporaries, and only served to show the poverty of invention of those who perpetrated them. (An exception must be made in the case of Stravinsky many of whose so-called 'neo-classic' works have much to commend them, the composer's originality and powers of invention usually effacing all traces of the original model. The music he wrote for the ballet *Pulcinella*, allegedly based on Pergolesi, is a good example of his skill in preserving eighteenth-century stylistic characteristics under a twentieth-century disguise.)

Somewhat akin to the neo-classic school, though starting from rather different premisses, were the advocates of a purely utilitarian approach to music, who maintained that the output of music should be regulated strictly in accordance with the law of supply and demand, just like any other commodity. The German composer, Paul Hindemith (1895–1963) was the principal exponent of this school of thought, and the kind of music he claimed to be able to provide was known as 'Gebrauchs', or 'Utility' music. The idea of a composer composing for his own satisfaction was ruled out by Hindemith and his followers as being no longer compatible with modern conditions. Consequently a great part of his earlier output consisted of *ad hoc* compositions written for all kinds of specific purposes—e.g., the training of children, or to provide professionals and amateurs with new material to play (as in the series of 'Kammermusik' written for different solo instruments in conjunction with small orchestras of varied character). Music written for films could also be considered as a kind of *Gebrauchsmusik*. This 'functional' conception of art is not, of course, a new one; in the pre-romantic era it was commonly accepted and some of the greatest music, for example, the Brandenburg Concertos and Church Cantatas of Bach, and a great many of Mozart's and Haydn's compositions, were written expressly in response to a definite demand. But with the coming of the romantic era, and the new conception of the artist as a rebel working outside, and often against, society, the pendulum swung to the opposite extreme, and the door was open to all kinds of eccentricities since now every 'artist' felt free to express himself and, in so doing, to invent, if necessary, a new vocabulary. Examples that come to mind are Scriabin with his 'mystical' chord, Haba with his quarter-tones, and Nicholas Oboukhov (1892–1954) a Russian composer of mystical leanings who, besides inventing a harmonic system of his own in which all the notes of the chromatic scale can be sounded at once, went further, and used to weep and howl and whistle and sneeze while interpreting his own compositions. Incidentally, the introduction of pure noise into musical scores, a device very popular with avant-garde contemporary composers, is no new thing; there are plenty of instances to be found in music composed since 1900. Richard Strauss, for example, introduces the cracking of whips into the score of *Elektra*; Darius Milhaud does the same with the addition of hammers and whistles in his *Choéphores*; Igor Markevitch (b. 1912) directs the wind players in his *Icare* to detach their mouth-pieces and blow into them; the French-American Edgard Varèse (1885–1965) built up vast tonal frescoes which are, in the last resort, nothing but noise intensified to the nth power; Alexander Mossolov (b. 1900) has imitated mechanical saws in a steel foundry, and Honegger the panting of a locomotive; the Brazilian Villa-Lobos (1887–1959) introduced the ticking of metronomes into one of his scores, while Erik Satie, as we have seen, used motor-horns, revolvers, sirens, Morse apparatus and typewriters in *Parade*.

It was perhaps inevitable, after all the ferment and extravagances of the 'twenties (which were, nevertheless, a period of intense creative activity in many fields) that the decade immediately preceding the second world war should have been marked by a certain relaxation of tension and the emergence of a new generation of musicians in France who felt that the time had come to restore to music some of the dignity and prestige it had seemed in danger of losing. Thus there came into being in 1936 the group 'Jeune France', founded with the intention of laying greater stress on the deeper human and spiritual values which composers of the post-first-world-war generation had tended rather to ignore. It was perhaps typical that they enjoyed the patronage of men like Paul Valéry, François Mauriac and Georges Duhamel in contrast to 'Les Six' whose sponsors at the time were distinctly lighter weight, more likely to be social than intellectual celebrities. The founders of 'Jeune France' were Olivier Messiaen, André Jolivet, Daniel Lesur and Yves Baudrier. Their aim was to bring music back into contact with life—in other words, to re-humanise it—in reaction against the somewhat frivolous approach of the 'Six', at least in their early works, who had certainly succeeded in rejuvenating music in one sense, but in such a way that it was in danger of becoming a mere 'divertissement', developing as it were, in a vacuum, without any real relevance to life, and out of touch with ordinary human emotions and aspirations. The actual founder and theoretician of the Group was Yves Baudrier (b. 1906) who, like Daniel Lesur (b. 1908) was opposed to any kind of system of theoretical research which they considered could only lead to the de-humanisation of music and consequent divorce between composer and public. In this they differed from Messiaen and Jolivet who did not consider that the cultivation of a particular method or technique of composition was in any way incompatible with the ideals they had in common—namely, the 'humanisation' of music. For them this could only be brought about considering music to be an aspect of the cosmos to which man belongs, and which should therefore be reflected in his music. The lines on which Messiaen developed his theories we shall be considering in a later chapter; in the meantime the importance of Jolivet (b. 1905), who was at one time a pupil of Messiaen and today one of France's most distinguished composers, must not be overlooked.

He studied for some years with Edgard Varèse and was soon initiated into the twelve-note technique practised by Schoenberg and Berg. Although not an orthodox dodecaphonist,

Jolivet decided at an early stage not only to liberate himself from tonality, as he put it, but to restore to music its primitive character which he conceives to have been a form of magic. Indeed, the notion of music being a form of *entertainment*, to give pleasure to an *audience*, who would *pay* to hear it, is a comparatively recent one in the history of the art; and did not exist until at least the late seventeenth or early eighteenth century. For as Professor Jacques Chailley is at pains to point out in his *40,000 Years of Music*[1]—'For primitive man music is not an art, it is a force. . . . Music is the only particle of the divine essence which men have been able to capture, and this has enabled them by means of prescribed rites, to identify themselves with the gods and exercise control over them. Then the process was reversed. After the gods have spoken to men through music, men through music will speak to the gods. Instead of subjugating them, they will now praise and flatter and pray to them. Through music they will have power over fate and the elements and animals. Sometimes too, when they are alone, they will use for their own purposes some of the marvellous powers of this supernatural language. . . . Music viewed as a spontaneous emanation from the human heart, is in a sense utilitarian and functional. It has no "public", and does not expect one. Its only public is the mysterious force to which it is addressed. The magical power of music is not a fable invented by mythomaniacs. It is with and through music that the African witch-doctor today forms his diagnoses and chases away the evil spirits; and in our countryside the village "witch", when she casts her spells to bring sickness to her neighbour's cow, often does so in a song; while in the innocent rhyming tags which children sing to decide who's going to be "out", the ethnologists have long ago detected the unconscious survival of the primitive magic by which we were once surrounded: song to begin with, then gradually only the spoken word. . . . Thus playing and singing were not artistic activities, but a sacred rite or religious function. When the musician was

[1] Paris 1961, London and New York 1964.

not alone but surrounded by people listening to him, the music's magic current did not flow from the musician to his audience, as it does with us today, but just the opposite: it was the musician who received from his hearers the impulse which caused him to reflect their feelings and emotions: he was, in the strict and noble sense of the word, an *interpreter*. . . .'

The same idea has been developed by Professor Wilfrid Mellers in his *Caliban Reborn: Renewal in twentieth-century music*,[1] especially in connexion with the music of the East which comes within the category he describes as Revelation, as distinct from what he calls 'the post-Renaissance doctrine of Incarnation'— or, in other words, 'music as magic as contrasted with music as expression'. In the music of India this trance-like quality is especially noticeable: 'when the Indian *vina* player takes up his instrument it is not to "put over" his own personality; the drone, which is eternity, hums continuously the music of the spheres', while the rhythmic organisation 'tends to be incantatory and hypnotic . . . and this unconsciousness of our earth and Time-bound condition is precisely the magic effect that primitive man sought through his music'.

It was this conception of music as a cosmic force that caused Jolivet to seek his inspiration in the more primitive forms of religion which find their expression in magical incantations, and it is this that gives to all his production a peculiar intensity rarely found elsewhere in contemporary music. The very titles of his works are an indication of the trend of his musical thought and of his constant preoccupation with those unseen forces whose vibrations he seeks to capture, for example: *Cosmogonie, Incantations, Danses rituelles, Mana*—this last title being the term that denotes, in primitive magic, that force which may connect a human being with some inanimate object considered as his fetish. Jolivet gave this title to a set of six pieces for the piano, composed in 1935, each of which is dedicated to some little familiar object of wood or metal standing

[1] London 1968.

on his writing-table whose inner essence, or 'Mana', is supposed to be conveyed in the music.[1]

The musical language of Jolivet is characterised by a certain harshness at times, no doubt to some extent inherited from his former teacher Varèse, and a feeling of tension. It is by and large atonal, but not strictly twelve-tone or serial, although he has on occasions written serial music, but without, as so many composers do, drawing attention to the fact. Jolivet is above all a genuinely creative artist and in all his works one feels that he has something to say that is of value, that compels our attention and is likely to move us emotionally. He has never, unlike some of his younger contemporaries, renounced all human feeling or been led by purely intellectual curiosity to pursue abstraction for its own sake.

In his capacity as musical director of the Comédie Française, Jolivet has written incidental music for a number of classical productions at that theatre; an opera on a book by Henri Ghéon: *Dolores ou le Miracle de la Femme Laide*; an Oratorio; three symphonies and various symphonic poems and a number of Concertos for various instruments, including one for Ondes Martenot, two for trumpet, one for percussion and perhaps the best known of all, the Concerto for piano and orchestra (1949), in which he incorporates elements borrowed from exotic sources: Africa in the first movement, the Far-East in the second and Polynesia in the third. As one French critic has

---

[1] It is interesting to note that Jules Combarieu, the first university professor in France since the Revolution to be officially appointed to teach the History of Music at the Collège de France, published in 1909 a work entitled *La Musique et la Magie* in which he laid down as an axiom that: 'The origins of music can be traced to man's anxiety in the face of the hostility of Nature which he interprets as being due to savage spirits who have to be appeased with incantations which can be used both as an offensive and a defensive weapon . . .; the development of the primitive incantation into a religious and socially organised lyrical form, and the gradual growth, by a process of abstraction, of an art cultivated for itself purely for recreative purposes—these are the three phases of evolution on which, in every country, a plan for a history of music can be based.'

pointed out,[1] in adopting this plan Jolivet had no 'picturesque' or documentary intentions: 'His aim was to establish a compromise between the traditional language of the tropical countries and current tendencies in our own Western music. In so doing he has deliberately emphasised the phenomenon of the 'Orientalisation' of Western music introduced more or less instinctively by Debussy (who in doing so has enlarged our understanding of Western music) and carried still further, notably in the music of Béla Bartók. In attempting to integrate two separate traditions—the European and the primitive-tropical—and to discover an aesthetic basis common to both, Jolivet has tried to create a universal language which would be practically accessible to European, Black and Yellow races alike. In this respect he has gone still further than Bartók in his latest works whose language, though truly universal, is yet only intended for a Western cultured élite.'

Jolivet is undoubtedly an important figure in French music today. He stands for freedom without licence, boldness without eccentricity and, because for him music is a language and not a code (as with so many avant-garde composers today) he uses it to establish communication between human beings and those unseen forces whose fluids he is able, magician-wise, to capture and transmit to those who have ears to hear.

Another outstanding figure, of an earlier generation than Jolivet's but who, like him, stands somewhat in a class apart, is the distinguished composer, theoretician and critic, Georges Migot (b. 1891). Migot, who has sometimes been referred to as the 'Group of One', is also a painter, engraver, writer, philosopher and pedagogue—a combination, in the words of one critic, of saint, savant and artisan. Religious by temperament and having made a special study of medieval music, he makes no concessions to fashion, but pursues only his own ideals. What those ideals are can perhaps best be explained in his own words, which are the expression of his aesthetic, philosophical and mystical creed: 'Over and above the

[1] Claude Rostand in *Petit Guide de l'auditeur de musique*.

aesthetic aspect of my works which is their tangible form, the materialisation of their spirituality, I obey the promptings of a fervent impulse, an ineffable ritual, an Agency, a Power which enables me to transmit through my work the secret and sacred message to those whose understanding penetrates deeply below the surface. This is not an intellectual conception such as some profess, but a spiritual one: *Spiritus*, transcending all subjective sensorial or sentimental conceptions, but without repudiating subject, senses or sentiment . . . I am both 'myst' and mystic, serving at the same time Love and Knowledge . . . I believe in continuous melodic lines superimposed, and architectural forms. (The fugue is not the only one.) Harmony is only the dress of a period which changes with every epoch. The only unchanging elements are line and form, melody and architecture which are revealed through Love and Knowledge.'

Migot's output which is considerable, includes large choral works, such as *Le Sermon sur la montagne, Psalm XIX*, the *a cappella* Oratorio *Saint Germain d'Auxerre* for four soloists and three mixed choirs, as well as operas and ballets, chamber music, songs and piano works, in all of which a certain archaic flavour is discernible, though his music is never academic. Such 'medievalism' as it contains is shown in the generally polyphonic character of the writing and its emphasis on line and melody rather than on harmony and colour. His music cannot be said to be in any sense typical of what is being written in France today (and in any case he belongs to an older generation), but because he is to this extent a lonely figure he merits a special mention. (A fuller account of his works will be found in Chapter 10.)

Although we are considering in this chapter the contribution of composers who were already prominent during the nineteen-thirties, many of these, of course, are either living today or at any rate continued to be active after the war. Into this category come composers like Henri Sauguet (b. 1901) and Florent Schmitt (1870–1958). In the case of Schmitt, however, most of his important works were written before the 1939 war, although he lived well on into the post-war period. He was a prolific composer, an 'Independent' belonging to no 'school' or group, whose output covers almost every domain, including incidental music for the theatre (notably his score for Gide's production of *Anthony and Cleopatra* at the Paris Opera in 1920); the ballet entitled *La tragédie de Salomé* (1907); various large-scale choral and orchestral works (of which the setting of *Psalm XLVII* is generally considered to be his masterpiece); numerous songs and piano pieces, and an important body of chamber music and other concerted works for solo instruments and orchestra. His Quintet for piano and string quartet (1908), a work of enormous complexity and great length, is typical of his tendency to over-elaborate, but is also a fine example of his generous lyrical expansiveness and technical accomplishment. Schmitt, who was born in Lorraine, was a pupil of Massenet and Fauré for composition at the Paris Conservatoire, and won the Grand Prix de Rome with his cantata *Semiramis* in 1900. His first Symphony, written in 1958 in the last year of his life at the age of 88, exhibits all the characteristics of his mature style, and provided a fitting close to the career of a gifted musician who, though not a composer of outstanding originality, worthily represented French music, if not at the most exalted level, for well over half a century.

The same could almost be said of Henri Sauguet who made his *début* as a member of Erik Satie's so-called Ecole d'Arcueil in 1923. Born in Bordeaux, Henri Poupard, as he was then (he later adopted his mother's name) showed an early interest in music, and after studying at Montauban with Joseph Canteloube (1879–1957), who had been a pupil of d'Indy, returned to Bordeaux where as a young man of nineteen he organised concerts of contemporary music, including works by Stravinsky, Schoenberg and the 'Six'. In 1921 he went to Paris at the invitation of Milhaud, to whom he had shown some of his earliest compositions, to hear Schoenberg's *Pierrot Lunaire*. By the following year he had settled in Paris, earning his living by day behind the counter of a big drapery store and studying under Charles Koechlin in the evenings. He made his public *début* with his one-act *opéra-bouffe Le Plumet du Colonel* (words and music by Henri Sauguet) commissioned and produced by the singer Madame Bériza at one of her concerts at the Théâtre des Champs-Elysées in April 1924. He was now set on a career during which he has always been faithful to his belief that, in the last resort, at the heart of all music there must be a core of melody and an element of mystery and poetic simplicity. Sauguet's music, like Poulenc's, has charm and elegance and wit, and a freshness and spontaneity that make it readily accessible. Among his best-known works are the ballets *La Chatte* (1927, commissioned by Diaghilev) and *Les Forains* (1945) a pathetic drama of strolling players written in collaboration with Boris Kochno, Roland Petit and Christian Bérard and dedicated to his old master Satie, the composer of *Parade*, the first ballet to have a fair-ground as its setting. In 1939 one of his major works, the opera based on Stendhal's *La Chartreuse de Parme* was produced at the Paris Opera after the composer had been working on it for ten years. His aim, he wrote at the time, was 'to write a work which, while remaining true to the spirit of Stendhal, would be the expression of my own sensibility and imagination in relation to the characters so tenderly cherished by the author'.

During the Occupation Sauguet expressed his horror of the war in his *Symphonie expiatoire* which he dedicated to the war's 'innocent victims'; and among his post-war works the most important are the opera *Les Caprices de Marianne* (1954), the Concerto for violin and orchestra (1953), *Le Cornette* (settings of nineteen poems by Rilke for bass and orchestra 1951) and the cantata on a poem by Jean Cayrol *L'Oiseau a vu tout cela* (1960) in which Sauguet's music highlights the pathos and horror of the theme—man's brutality to man observed through the eyes of a bird—in discreet yet moving accents. It is with works of this calibre as well as with so many others in his varied output in which a just balance is preserved between wit and elegance on the one hand and a candid emotional sensibility on the other, that Sauguet has ensured for himself a place among the most significant composers of his generation in France.

Other 'middle of the road' composers who were active in the nineteen-thirties were Jacques Ibert (1890–1962), Jean Françaix (b. 1912), Jean Rivier (b. 1896) and Maurice Jaubert (1900–1940). It has been reckoned that there were in the period between the wars about one hundred French composers whose works were quoted, so to speak, on the musical stock exchange, only a few of whom belonged to some group or were directly associated with some tendency or 'school'. The remainder were, for the most part, 'independents' on whom it would be as difficult to pin a label as they themselves would have been reluctant to accept one. There can therefore be no question, within the limits of this chapter, of attempting to list still less to comment at length on all the personalities in this 'musicians' gallery'. Suffice it to say that Ibert, sometime Director of the Villa Medici (seat in Rome of the French Academy) excelled in a light yet classical vein and was the author of seven light operas (notably *Angélique* and *Le Roi d'Yvetot*), and a number of symphonic works of which *Escales* enjoyed great popularity at one time; Jean Françaix writes attractive light-weight music in a neo-classic vein; while Rivier has the distinction of being the author of five symphonies as well as an opera, writing music neither revolutionary nor reactionary but using freely the modern idiom.

The case of Maurice Jaubert is the tragic one of a composer of great promise meeting an untimely death before his personality and talent could find their full expression. At the age of nineteen Jaubert, who was born in Nice, was the youngest practising barrister in France with a brilliant career before him. Concurrently he was studying music at the Nice Conservatoire, and by the time he was twenty-three he had made a fateful decision: music, not law, would be his profession. Encouraged by Honegger in Paris, Jaubert was soon launched on his new career, and presently became musical director of Pathé Films, writing the music for some forty films, notably for Margaret Kennedy's *The Constant Nymph*, *Altitude 3,200*, *Carnet de bal* and René Clair's *Le dernier milliardaire*. His symphonic music included *Cantate pour le temps pascal*, *La chanson de Tessa* (from *The Constant Nymph*) for voice and orchestra, and a 'symphonie concertante' for soprano and orchestra on Charles Péguy's poem *Jeanne d'Arc*. When war broke out in 1939 Jaubert served as a captain in the Engineers, and was killed in 1940 while blowing up a bridge under heavy fire.

He was one of those composers, typical of this generation, who had no desire to be 'modish' or even self-consciously 'modern', as later became the fashion, and his music owes nothing to any schools or dogmas, conforming rather to the ideals proclaimed by Honegger who used to say that when music loses contact with the masses it renounces its special privilege, which is to radiate. . . . 'An art which is to survive must appeal to the emotions ('la sensibilité') though it need not ignore new conquests in language and instrumentation. One can express feeling without being banal, and be progressive without becoming incomprehensible. To ask whether this is easy is beside the point. Nothing in art is easy.'

This rational, non-extremist point of view was certainly more in evidence during the nineteen-thirties than it had been in the previous decade. The stir created by the pranks of 'Les Six' in their early days, when one of their aims was admittedly to shock academic and bourgeois circles by playing down the 'serious' side of music, was now almost forgotten, and the members of the group had themselves settled down and were by now pursuing independent paths. Honegger with his *Jeanne d'Arc au bûcher*, and Milhaud with his two large-scale operas, *Christophe Colomb* and *Maximilien*, were now launched as 'serious composers'; Poulenc had written some of his best music, for example the Mass, *Litanies à la Vierge Noire* and the song-cycle *Tel jour, telle nuit*; while Auric had made a highly successful *début* as an outstanding composer of film music with *A nous la liberté*, and was now writing serious musical criticism

Darius Milhaud, 1892–

Jean Cocteau, 1889–1963

Henri Sauguet, 1901–

in the Paris press. Meanwhile, the big names at the top were still those of Roussel, Koechlin and Dukas and, of course, Ravel; though after 1932 until his death in 1937 the voice of the composer of *Daphnis et Chloë* had been silenced by the incurable illness that had clouded his last years.

Looking back in retrospect on the nineteen-thirties, the period can be seen as a kind of interregnum, an uneasy lull between the hectic 'twenties and the more radically progressive epoch that opened after the second world war. Politically these were uneasy and unstable years. The gradual rise to power of Hitler, and the savage civil war in Spain were disquieting evidence that sinister forces were at work and that the peace of the world was in danger once again. By 1940 mankind's worst fears had become a reality, and during the next five years' struggle to save what remained of civilisation the arts inevitably stagnated. When they were revived at the conclusion of the war they entered a new phase, and music especially was destined to undergo a more radical transformation than it had ever experienced in the past. Indeed, from 1945 until the present day, the vocabulary and language of music has been immeasurably extended, sometimes to the point of incoherence. This enlargement of the boundaries of an art which throughout the centuries had always been one of the most conventionally regulated of all the arts is, of course, a consequence of the abolition of the notion of tonality, which inevitably led to the removal of the last barriers between music, hitherto considered to be the art of ordered sound, and noise, which is sound in the raw, as yet untamed and ignoring harmony.

This trend, it is true, was first manifested before the first world war in the works of Schoenberg and his followers; but it is a far cry from the strictly controlled and didactic atonality of the Viennese school in those days to the deliberately anarchic excesses of a few avant-garde extremists in the nineteen-sixties who, in the apparent absence of any talent for or interest in music as such, preferred to exercise their ingenuity in devising new ways of manipulating disagreeable sounds.

One of the few pioneers in this field between the two wars, though fundamentally a serious musician and in no sense a charlatan, was the Franco-American composer Edgard Varèse (1885–1965) of whom something should be said at this juncture as he was one of the first, in France at any rate, to experiment with sound as such, both before and after the 1939 war. Varèse was born in France of mixed French and Italian parentage, and became an American citizen in 1927. He was a pupil of Vincent d'Indy and Albert Roussel at the Schola Cantorum, and also of the famous organist and composer Charles-Marie Widor (1845–1937) at the Paris Conservatoire; and it was on the recommendation of Widor and Massenet that he was awarded at the age of nineteen a scholarship, granted by the Paris Municipality. In France he was encouraged by Debussy, who corresponded with him until his departure for the United States in 1916; and we hear of Varèse conducting the *Martyre de Saint Sébastien* and other little-known modern French works in Prague in 1914. While in Berlin in the pre-war years Varèse became a close friend and pupil of Busoni whose theories, notably those expounded in his *New Aesthetic of Music*, had a great influence on his future development. In New York Varèse founded the *International Composers' Guild*, and organised first performances in America of works by Satie, Honegger, Poulenc, Milhaud, Bartók, Malipiero, Hindemith, Webern, Berg and Schoenberg, and it was in New York that three of the works, in which he first gave expression to his new vision of music conceived in terms of timbre, pitch, dynamics, rhythm and what he called the 'spatial organisation of sound' from which melody and harmony, in the accepted sense of the terms, were rigorously excluded had their first performance. These were: *Offrandes*, *Octandre* and *Hyperprism* composed in 1922–4. Acknowledging the encouragement he received from Busoni, Varèse declared that 'he had the gift of stimulating my mind, opening before me gulfs of prophetic imagination. I became a sort of diabolical Parsifal seeking not the Holy Grail, but a bomb which would blow up the world of music and let in all kinds of sounds—sounds which at that time were classed as noise.'

To obtain his effects Varèse relied mainly on wind instruments and percussion. *Ionisation*, for example, is for 35 percussion instruments including anvils and sirens; while in *Déserts* (1954) he employs, in addition to 14 woodwind and brass instruments, 47 instruments of percussion as well as a piano and two magnetic tapes of 'organised sound' reproducing noises recorded in factories, and processed electronically. Here, to some extent, Varèse is adopting the theory of the Futurists (see Chapter 2) to the effect that in so far as the noises that surround us in street and factory are part of modern life they should be reflected in the arts—not only in music, but in painting and literature as well—; but whereas Russolo envisaged an orchestra of 'Bruiteurs'—instruments designed to produce specific noises such as humming, whistling, groaning, gurgling, etc.—Varèse used conventional instruments, but in an unconventional way, and organised his sound structures with the skill of a trained musician with the object of enlarging the boundaries of music without abolishing music itself.

His career falls into two distinct creative periods—before and after the war of 1939. One of his last works was the *Poème électronique* written, at the request of the architect Le Corbusier, designer of the Philips Pavilion at the Brussels Exhibition of 1958. It necessitated 400 loudspeakers, and was one of the sensations of the Exhibition. It was his response to Le Corbusier's request for 'a poem of the electronic age' which would put the audience 'in the presence of the genesis of the world'. For a man of seventy this was a remarkable achievement, showing that the urge to push the boundaries of music to their extremest limits, which had possessed him all his life, was still as potent in his old age as it had been in his youth. Equally remarkable is the fact that he could claim to be the first composer of the century to conceive of music in these terms; for what he was already doing in the nineteen-twenties was an entirely new departure, something quite different from the purely intellectual a-tonalism and serialism of Schoenberg and his followers. Varèse was primarily concerned with sound as such; for, as one contemporary critic has very pertinently pointed out,[1] 'There is in his scores no harmonic integration of one part with another, no thematic development; simply the placing together of sound-blocks . . . In seeking freedom from the established norms, the "arbitrary restrictions" as he calls them, of musical expression, Varèse found himself in a sort of aesthetic no-man's land, where the frontiers that separate music from the other arts are ill-defined. Clearly, if you reject as a basis of composition all the conventional devices of your craft you must look elsewhere for something to take their place. Varèse looked to the visual arts, to sculpture and architecture . . . he blurs the distinction between time and space; his pieces are given geometrical titles, for instance *Hyperprism* and *Octandre*, and his sound-patterns are the musical equivalent of that Futurism, Cubism, Primitivism that we associate in painting and sculpture with the work of Braque, Picasso, Giacometti, Moore. . . . Varèse rejected the Impressionistic use of sound; instead, he made sounds intrinsic to the structure.' The same writer, after suggesting a parallel between the theories of Varèse with regard to the 'identification of a man with his inner nature as well as with his outer environment' and the philosophy of Existentialism, observes that Varèse 'does not seek to assert the human will so much as to submit it to the timeless void that is Nature. We move through a waste-land of sound; this or that feature is made prominent. Does Varèse succeed in impressing us with his "meaning and purpose"? There is no doubt of the disturbing relevance of his work, nor of its influence on later composers of the avant-garde, both because of the finer points of his technique, and because of the broad scope of his quest.'

It is true, of course, that Varèse has been a force to reckon

[1] See Francis Routh: *Contemporary music: an Introduction*, English Universities Press Ltd. 1968.

with in latter-day developments in contemporary music, and that certain procedures favoured by some extremist composers today are directly traceable to his influence and initiative; and whatever view we may take as to the validity of his aesthetic ideals or the intrinsic value of his music, credit is due to him as one of the great pioneers in the 'emancipation' of music with which so many twentieth-century composers in France have been concerned, each in their different ways, from Debussy down to the present day. In the years immediately following the last war many developments have taken place, and it is these we have now to consider.

CHAPTER NINE

MESSIAEN, BOULEZ AND AFTER

The conflagration of 1939–45, though less sanguinary than that of 1914–18, had repercussions of a moral and psychological nature which have left their mark on all the nations involved. These war years—and, in the case of France, the Occupation—must be held responsible for certain deviations and distortions in the arts and a deliberate cult of eccentricity and sensationalism, sometimes pushed to extremes which have no artistic justification whatever. In the case of music the tendency in some quarters is to do everything possible to dehumanise and de-personalise it by the substitution wherever possible of mechanical sound devices, such as electronic vibrations or magnetic tapes of artificially distorted sounds (concrete music) to take the place of instruments or the natural human voice. Some composers leave everything to chance or to the computer; some would reduce music to a haphazard succession of isolated sounds, or even to silence.

These are, of course, extreme cases; but they do raise the whole question of the position of the artist in society and, in the case of music, the composer-audience relationship which, never very clearly defined, is complicated and obscured today by the gulf that tends to grow wider all the time between the creative musician and his public. This is due to a variety of causes, mainly social or psychological. In the first place the changing structure of society, accelerated in a country such as France by the after effects of the war and enemy occupation, and aggravated by international tension and general political unrest, must have an inhibiting effect on artists and intellectuals. In the second place there is the purely psychological, or rather aesthetic problem, with which every creative artist is confronted today, namely the necessity of 'making a choice'. It may well seem to the young composer as he sits down before his blank sheet of manuscript paper that everything has been said already, all styles and modes have been tried out, every technical device, every orchestral effect employed and that, short of inventing a new language, there is nothing left for him to do. Hence the cynicism, disillusionment and scepticism of so much contemporary music. Where there is no faith there can be no genuine creation. This explains, too, the modern preoccupation with purely technical processes, 'systems' of composition and the like which are elaborated and put into practice with a supreme disregard for the sensibilities of the listener. Thus there is a real danger that the composer may soon find himself working in a vacuum, cut off from all contacts with the ordinary musical public and as effectively isolated from the outside world of normal human beings as the atomic scientist in the inner recesses of his laboratory.

It is this problem—the problem of the composer-listener relationship—that has become so acute in almost every country today that, unless some solution is found, the musicians will end by speaking a language that no one can understand outside a small circle of initiates, and the public will respond by unjustly and indiscriminately condemning *all* contemporary art and sinking back into an apathetic and complacent but uncritical admiration of the past. Composers will then either starve or take up other pursuits until the next genius comes along with an 'Open Sesame' which will break down those barriers against which both artists and public have for so long been battering in vain, from opposite sides, without ever succeeding in communicating with one another. But with the arrival of a new musical genius, who can say what miracles might be worked? It is the coming of this musical Messiah that may perhaps rescue European music from itself. As Darius Milhaud once said: 'La musique de l'avenir sera celle que le prochain musicien de génie écrira.' Is the world waiting today for such a genius to appear? or are there those who maintain that he is already here? This is a leading question to which there must be as many answers as there are schools of thought, and one which can perhaps best be left to posterity to decide.

There have, of course, always been in France plenty of gifted musicians who, as we have seen, have preserved their independence and refused to bind themselves to any 'system', whether 'twelve-note' or any other. It is a curious fact, however, that it was only after the last war that a number of young composers suddenly discovered 'serial' music and under the guidance of Arnold Schoenberg's leading disciple, René Leibowitz (b. 1913), began assiduously to adopt the 'twelve-note' technique invented by Schoenberg in Vienna and first used by him in his opus 23 in 1923. Schoenberg described his system as 'a method of composition with twelve notes related only to each other', because it was based entirely on the notes of the chromatic scale, twelve in number. Such music (and this applies to nearly all music written today, whether 'serial' or not) is also necessarily a-tonal, since it repudiates tonality, that is to say the traditional diatonic scale, with its tonic and dominant, which has been the basis of Western music for the last three or four hundred years. It is claimed that the excessive chromaticism of late nineteenth-century composers, such as Liszt and Wagner, had already outstepped the bounds of traditional harmony (which is true), and that a scale entirely composed of twelve semitones, with no such fixed points of tension and contrast as are implied in the old 'tonic' and 'dominant' relationship, was bound to be the next step in the emancipation of musical speech (which may or may not be true). Where the theory runs counter to the whole tradition of Western music is that, whereas in the latter what constitutes a theme has always been determined by the natural relationships and affinities between one note and another, in serial music it depends merely on the *numerical* order in which the notes occur. This is because, in the absence of 'key', and consequently of any possibility of tonal contrasts through modulation, the only way for an atonal composer to achieve variety or a shape of any kind is to group his notes in series. That is to say, they must be played in an unvarying order to begin with, although after the first statement the 'theme' can be twisted back on itself, turned upside down, played backwards and made to undergo every sort of transformation that ingenuity can devise, provided that the original 'series' of notes is always respected.

This is not, of course, to imply that masterpieces, or near masterpieces have not been written in this idiom by composers who, like the great Viennese Triumvirate, have found it temperamentally congenial and a real aid to self-expression. What does seem surprising, however, is that what might well have been only a temporary fashion, a discipline which, like Cubism in painting, would help to purge modern music of some of its extravagances, should, after being more or less abandoned on the Continent in the years immediately preceding the second world war, have been taken up again in France in the post-war years by the younger generation of present-day composers.

Today, of course, the situation has changed, and serialism after having been extended to apply to almost every aspect of musical structure—pitch, duration, intensity, etc.—resulting in scores of immense complexity to the eye if often unintelligible to the ear, has now been more or less discarded by the avant-garde in favour of other equally cerebral theories and techniques. It is nevertheless necessary at this point to look backwards to the years immediately following the war to see the situation as it was then in France, and to give some account of current trends and of the new generation of composers who represent their country today.

Of these the most influential, both as trend-setters and as individuals, have been Olivier Messiaen (b. 1908) and Pierre Boulez (b. 1925); and most of the younger men who have followed them owe a great deal to their training and example. Messiaen especially has had an enormous influence on a whole generation of musicians, directly through his teaching at the Paris Conservatoire, and indirectly through the impact made by his works in which he seems to have discovered, if not a new musical language, at least a new dimension. What distinguishes his music from that of other contemporary composers is, above all, its extraordinary blend of cerebrality and sensuality, of violence and insipidity all wrapped up in an elaborate web of rhythmic and harmonic complexities not always immediately intelligible to the ear. A feature of his music is the use he makes of exact transcriptions of bird-song and of Oriental modes and metric patterns, mainly Hindu or Ancient Greek. He has made a profound study of rhythm in all its aspects, and has embodied his theories on this and all other features of his highly individual methods of composition in his two-volume treatise: *La technique de mon langage musical*, published in 1953. Another key-work which has had important repercussions is a piano piece, introduced at Darmstadt in 1949, entitled *Modes de valeur et d'intensités*. In this exercise Messiaen demonstrates how the principle of serialisation can be rigidly applied, not only to the notes in a twelve-tone row, but to all the parameters of pitch, duration, intensity, attack, etc., as well—a procedure which many avant-garde composers, notably Boulez, Stockhausen and others lost no time in adopting, and in doing so sounded the death-knell of strict Schoenberg serialism which was rapidly becoming a merely academic formula.

The career of the composer who could fairly be said to have inaugurated a new era in French music has not been externally spectacular in any way. Olivier Messiaen came from a literary family; his father was a professor of English, the author of an annotated translation of the complete works of Shakespeare, while his mother was a well-known poetess who wrote under the name of Cécile Sauvage. He taught himself the piano during the 1914 war, and made his first attempts at composition, notably a setting of Tennyson's *The Lady of Shalott*. In 1919 he entered the Paris Conservatoire, and studied, among others, with Marcel Dupré, Maurice Emmanuel and Paul Dukas. On leaving the Conservatoire in 1931, after carrying off a number of first prizes, the young Messiaen was appointed organist of the church of La Trinité in Paris, a post which he has held ever since. In the same year his first published work for orchestra, *Les Offrandes oubliées*, described as a 'symphonic meditation' was performed for the first time in Paris at a public concert conducted by Walter Straram. In 1936 Messiaen was appointed to teaching posts at the Ecole Normale de Musique and at the Schola Cantorum; in the same year he founded, as already related, the group *Jeune France* together with André Jolivet, Daniel-Lesur and Yves Baudrier. When the war came in 1939, Messiaen was mobilised as a private soldier and taken prisoner the following year. This was, in some respects, a turning point in his career, for it was during his captivity in Stalag 8A in Silesia that he composed one of his most significant and important works—the *Quatuor pour la fin du Temps* for violin, clarinet, cello and piano which had its first performance before an audience consisting of 5000 prisoners of war.

On his return to Paris, Messiaen was appointed Professor of harmony at the Paris Conservatoire, and in 1943 he gave the first performance, partnered by Yvonne Loriod who was later to become his wife, of *Visions de l'Amen* for two pianos at a concert organised by La Pléiade. The following year saw the publication of his treatise *Technique de mon langage musical*, and in the spring of 1945 two of his best known works, *Vingt regards sur l'Enfant Jésus* and *Trois petites liturgies de la Présence Divine* (the latter under the direction of the late Roger Désormière) were performed for the first time in Paris. It was from this moment that Messiaen became a controversial figure after the somewhat hostile reception accorded to the *Trois petites liturgies*; the 'cas Messiaen' was now dividing public opinion.

The next important step in his career was his appointment in 1947 to take charge of a new class at the Conservatoire in 'Aesthetics, Analysis and Rhythm', which in the years to follow attracted young composers from all over the world and confirmed his reputation as an inspiring as well as erudite teacher.

During the next two years Messiaen went first to Italy, at the invitation of Luigi Dallapiccola, and then to the United States where he conducted a composition class at the Tanglewood Music Centre. It was here that one of his most remarkable works, the *Cinq Rechants* for unaccompanied choir, was given for the first time, to be followed later in the year by the first performance of one of the best known and most controversial of all Messiaen's works, the 'Turangalîla' Symphony, commissioned by Koussevitsky and performed by the Boston Symphony Orchestra under Leonard Bernstein. This extraordinary work is in ten movements and calls for an immense orchestra with, in addition to a normal string and wind section a formidable body of percussion instruments, a solo piano and 'Ondes Martenot'. The composer has given the following account of the work's instrumental organisation (the title, from the Hindu, means a 'Love-song'): 'The three keyboard instruments, glockenspiel, celesta and vibraphone, have a special part similar to that of an East Indian *gamelang* as used in Java and Bali. The percussion performs true rhythmic counterpoints. It comprises temple blocks, wood block, small cymbal, suspended cymbal, Chinese cymbal, gong, tambourine, triangle, maracas, side drums [with snares], bass drum and eight tubular bells. In addition, an "Onde Martenot" dominates the orchestra with its expressive voice. Finally, a part for pianoforte solo, which is extremely difficult, is designed to add brilliance to the orchestra, with chord clusters, and bird songs, thus making the "Turangalîla" Symphony almost a concerto for pianoforte and orchestra.' The theme the symphony is supposed to illustrate is the conflict between physical and spiritual love, and the work is the central panel of a triptych dealing with human passion forming what Messiaen has called his 'Tristan trilogy', the others being *Harawi* (1945), a song of love and death for soprano and piano on a text derived from Peruvian folklore, and the above-mentioned *Cinq Rechants* in praise of physical love, for which Messiaen himself wrote the words, with music derived partly from primitive sources including French troubadour refrains and Hindu and Peruvian folk song. In some of these songs the place of words is taken by onomatopaeic sounds which call for considerable virtuosity on the part of the singers. Messiaen now began to turn his attention to the organ, for which up to now, though himself a very fine organist, he had written nothing of particular importance. In 1950 he brought out his *Messe de la Pentecôte* for the instrument, and three years later gave the first performance at Stuttgart of his monumental *Livre d'Orgue*, one of the most remarkable and original contributions to the literature of the instrument in modern times. It was not until 1955 that the work was played by the composer for the first time in France in his own church of La Trinité in Paris.

Messiaen's preoccupation with bird-song, one of the essential ingredients of his compositional technique, now found its fullest expression in three characteristic works which are almost wholly bird-inspired: *Le Reveil des oiseaux* (1953) for piano and orchestra; *Oiseaux exotiques* (1955) for piano and chamber orchestra and the voluminous *Catalogue d'oiseaux* (1959) for piano solo which takes over an hour to perform and includes transcriptions decked out with every variety of pianistic and harmonic extravagance of bird-song culled from almost every country in the world. Many of these pieces have an almost symphonic quality and present the performer with formidable technical problems.

The year 1960 represents another stage in Messiaen's evolution, for it was marked by the production of one of his most important and controversial works, *Chronochromie* (The colour of Time) for orchestra, which had its first performance at the Donaueschingen Festival. The composer has given the following description of this vast symphonic fresco which he tells us 'is based on twofold materials—temporal, or rhythmic, and sonorous, or melodic. The former employs thirty-two different durations (i.e. from the demi-semiquaver to the breve) treated as symmetrical inversions and always inverted in the same order. . . . The sonorous material employs French, Swedish,

Japanese and Mexican bird-song. It also uses the sound of water (mountain streams and waterfalls noted in the French Alps). The blending of sounds and colours, which is very complex, remains at the disposal of the durations which they underline by colouring them. Colour thus serves to reveal the divisions of time.' Messiaen then goes on to describe how the 'durations are coloured by melodic counterpoints (French bird-song on the wood-wind and keyboard instruments); by three metallic timbres (gongs, bells, suspended cymbals, etc.); by stacks of chords in different colouring applied systematically to each permutation'.

It is interesting to speculate, as one French critic has suggested,[1] whether in choosing this title *Chronochromie* the composer was perhaps thinking of a remark Debussy once made to his publisher when he was working on the orchestral *Images* to the effect that 'music in its essence is not something that can be moulded into a rigorous and traditional form: it is a rhythmic expression of colour and time'. In any case, it is noteworthy that Messiaen, like Debussy, never writes music in any of the traditional forms—sonata, fugue, canon or any other ready-made mould.

There is in *Chronochromie* one extraordinary episode which, like the *Rite of Spring*, caused some disturbance when the work was first performed, so harshly does it fall upon the ear; and indeed, most audiences today find it difficult to take. The passage in question is scored for eighteen solo strings—twelve violins, four violas and two cellos—and consists of the songs of eighteen different species of birds treated contrapuntally in eighteen entirely independent parts. The composer admits that this passage creates an impression of chaotic and discordant confusion, but excuses it on the grounds that this apparent disorder conceals a hidden order, though this may only be perceptible to himself. In nature, as he points out, the sound of eighteen different species of bird singing together in

[1] See Jean Roy: *Musique française: présences contemporaines*, chapter on Olivier Messiaen.

the forest at dawn, for example, would not strike harshly on the ear; it is only when such sounds are transferred to instruments and transported to the concert-hall, divorced from their natural surroundings, that the result appears to be pure cacophony. This being so, it is surely open to question whether this attempt to incorporate the crude sounds of a bird chorus heard in the open air into a highly sophisticated musical structure, using conventional instruments whose timbre has nothing in common with the voice of a bird, can be considered an aesthetically valid procedure. Few composers would have taken the risk; for Messiaen there is nothing that cannot be expressed in terms of music, from religious ecstasy down to the humblest sound in Nature.

The structure of *Chronochromie* is immensely complex, involving elaborate mathematical calculations. For example, the composer describes how the 'Strophes' forming the most important part of the work are based on symmetrical permutations of the thirty-two time values between a demi-semiquaver and a breve; i.e., a series ranging from one to thirty-two demi-semiquavers with all the intermediate durations. When three lines of different permutations are heard simultaneously, Messiaen explains how the different note values are given a different colouring by associating them with instruments of different *timbres* and special combinations; e.g., woodwind, glockenspiel and xylophone for one line; gongs, bells and cymbals for another; and finally combinations of percussion and strings. Each time-value (duration) will be marked by a different colour: 'One by a sound suggesting red mixed with blue; another by a mixture of milk-white, orange and gold; another will be pale grey with green or violet reflections and so on. . . . Juxtaposed or superimposed, they will all be distinguished by their coloration, colour being used to distinguish divisions (découpages) of Time.' What is not so easy to explain is how the listener can be expected to distinguish aurally between all these devices, or to get the impression from them, especially those relating to colour, which exist solely in the composer's imagination. The work is nevertheless a technical *tour de force*, an impressive edifice of sound which must be considered one of Messiaen's most original and provocative creations.

It was followed after an interval of two years by the *Sept Haikai* written on the composer's return from a visit to Japan. Once again, the musical material is derived from bird-song, and the instruments specially chosen to represent the cries of a number of Japanese birds. The work is scored for eleven woodwind—flutes, oboes, cor anglais, clarinets of various kinds and two bassoons; one trumpet and one trombone; a marimba and a xylophone to represent some particularly brilliant warblers, and a solo piano playing five cadenzas, some based on bird-song, all of them intended as virtuoso pieces. In addition there is a complete orchestra of percussion instruments consisting of a set of cencerros, a set of *crotales* (small clappers), a triangle, eighteen tubular bells, two small Turkish cymbals, two gongs, a Chinese cymbal and two tam-tams. But this is not all. Eight violins are employed solely to produce the grating sound of the Japanese mouth-organ known as 'Shô'. The *Sept Haikai* had its first performance at a *Domaine Musical* concert in Paris in October 1963, under the direction of Pierre Boulez.

It was Boulez, too, who directed the first performance at Donaueschingen in 1964 of one of Messiaen's strangest works, entitled *Couleurs de la Cité Céleste*, written in response to a request from Dr. Heinrich Strobel for a piece scored for three trombones and three xylophones. This posed certain problems which Messiaen solved by combining with these instruments a piano, three clarinets, a small trumpet in D, three other trumpets and two horns in F and a bass trombone. But instead of three xylophones, he decided to use only one, combined with a xylorimba and a marimba adding, to complete his orchestration, a set of cencerros, a set of bells, four gongs and two tam-tams. The sound of trombones he associated with the Apocalypse (Book of Revelation), and this led him to seek in

Olivier Messiaen, 1908–

Pierre Boulez, 1925–

the Book suitable quotations around which to build this work which, as he has said, 'reflects my main preoccupations. First those of a religious nature since it is based on five quotations from the Apocalypse; and secondly my love of mystery, magic and fantasy, because these quotations from the Apocalypse are extraordinary, extravagant, surrealist and terrifying. . . . This has enabled me to imagine such effects as a combination of the low pedal notes on the trombone with the highest register of the three clarinets. Furthermore, the 'colours' in the title are the colours of Paradise.' Other ingredients in this piece are once again bird-song and Hindu and Greek rhythms and themes borrowed from Plainsong.

One of the most recent and important of Messiaen's large-scale works was commissioned by the French Minister of Fine Arts, André Malraux, and performed for the first time (privately) in the Sainte Chapelle in Paris in 1965. Entitled *Et exspecto resurrectionem mortuorum*, it is based on Biblical texts, notably the resurrection of Christ, and scored for eighteen woodwind, sixteen brass and a battery of percussion instruments. It had its second performance in the Cathedral of Chartres in the presence of General de Gaulle, and its first public performance under Pierre Boulez at a Domaine Musical concert in 1966. That same year Olivier Messiaen was appointed Professor at the Paris Conservatoire.[1]

What is unique about Messiaen's art in an age of unbelief is that it is an expression of his belief in God, his compassion for humanity and his love of Nature. It is through music that he seeks to exteriorise his religious beliefs as a devout Catholic, but his approach to his art is that of a mystic rather than a theologian. It is also a highly self-conscious approach, with a touch of theatricality about it that some may find disconcerting. To many, in fact, the mysticism of Messiaen seems too theatrical to be true, and the means he employs to create a

---

[1] A later work of similar religious inspiration is *La transfiguration de Notre Seigneur Jésus Christ*, for chorus, orchestra and small instrumental ensemble, first heard in England in July 1970.

celestial atmosphere seem sometimes to border on the mer-
etricious. At the same time, of course, he is a highly accomplished technician, always seeking to enlarge the boundaries
of musical speech though the quality of his thought, in purely
musical terms, is often undistinguished. One of the most disconcerting features of his music is, in fact, the contrast between
the immense complexity of the language and the often startling
banality of the underlying musical ideas. The effect of such
music on the listener is, however, unpredictable. The approach
on both sides, i.e., from the standpoint of the composer as well
as the listener, is too subjective. The latter's attitude is clearly
conditioned, to some extent at least, by the affirmation of faith
or feeling with which the composer accompanies almost every
note he sets on paper. This self-consciousness in the composer
finds an echo in the listener, who is bound to have a positive
reaction, either hostile or sympathetic, to such declarations as:
'All my works are an act of faith, and glorify the mystery of
Christ. In my inarticulate strivings to express the Divine Love,
I have tried to find music that will be the equivalent of a new
Time and a new Space—music that will love and sing. . . .'

Again, in a well-known and often quoted declaration, this is
how Messiaen describes the music which is his ideal: 'My preference is for music that is brilliant in texture, refined, even
voluptuous (but of course not sensual). Music that soothes and
that sings (all honour to melody and the melodic phrase!),
music that is like new blood, a signed gesture, an unknown
perfume, a never-sleeping bird. Music like stained glass, a
whirl of complementary colours. Music that expresses the end
of time, Ubiquity, the bodies of the saints and all divine and
supernatural mysteries. *A theological rainbow.*'

This is the language of emotion and exaltation which does
nothing to help an objective evaluation of Messiaen considered purely as a musician. In the last resort it is as a technician, theorist and craftsman, rather than as a poet, mystic and
theologian, that he must be judged—and there is no doubt that
he is today one of the most accomplished and erudite com-

posers now living, widely cultivated and an inspiring and influential teacher. Many of his theories with regard to rhythm,
modes, harmonies and all sorts of structural and formal procedures are both original and of real value; and in his search
for new modes of expression Messiaen has explored hitherto
uncharted regions of sound and rhythm, besides enriching the
palette of the modern orchestra by introducing all kinds of
novel instrumental effects. If there is a weak point in this remarkable and highly original composer's formidable equip-
ment, it is that in so many of his works the impressive nature
and importance of the vast instrumental machinery and technical *tours de force* set in motion seem too often to be out of all
proportion to the value of the musical ideas in themselves. It
is for this reason that in judging Messiaen's *œuvre* as a whole,
the verdict of posterity may well be that it has failed to
achieve that perfect synthesis of form and content which is the
hallmark of great art.

The influence of Messiaen as a teacher has, as we have seen,
been considerable over a whole generation of young musicians,
and of all those who have been his pupils at one time or another, the most distinguished today is undoubtedly Pierre
Boulez whom Messiaen himself has described as 'the greatest
musician of his generation, and perhaps of the last half-
century'. And, according to Antoine Goléa,[1] the story of
Boulez' apprenticeship is the story of the evolution of music
since the end of world war II. Born at Montbrison on the
Loire on 26 March 1925, he had his early schooling at the
Collège de St. Etienne where he specialised in mathematics as
his father was anxious for him to become an engineer. At the
same time he showed an interest in music and learned to play
the piano. Opportunities for hearing contemporary music in
the provinces were at that time few and far between, but it is
said that it was hearing a record of Stravinsky's *Rossignol* that
decided young Boulez to give up mathematics and take up
music as a profession. This meant a move to Paris where, in

[1] See *Esthétique de la musique contemporaine*, Paris 1954.

the last years of the war, he entered the Conservatoire and studied harmony in Olivier Messiaen's class where he had as fellow students Yvonne Loriod, Maurice Le Roux, Serge Nigg and Jean-Louis Martinet. After little more than a year at the Conservatoire Boulez left to study privately with René Leibowitz, a pupil of Schoenberg, who had come to Paris to preach the gospel of serialism to young composers, and learned from him the theory and practice of the so-called twelve-note technique. In 1946 Boulez was appointed director of music with the theatrical company newly formed by Jean-Louis Barrault and Madeleine Renaud, and in the same year made his official debut as a composer with three works: the Sonatine for flute and piano; the first Piano Sonata and the song-cycle *Le visage nuptial*, a setting of five poems by the surrealist poet René Char, for soprano, contralto, chorus and orchestra. It was again René Char who provided the text for Boulez' next important work, the cantata *Le soleil des eaux* (1948) for soprano, tenor, bass, chorus and orchestra; and this was followed in the same year by the second Piano Sonata, one of the most revolutionary of all his early works in which Boulez uncompromisingly 'serialises' not only themes and notes, but rhythm (treated as rhythmic cells) duration, pitch, intensity, etc. producing in this way a complex web of apparently incoherent sounds which, however, according to one contemporary critic, 'invite our participation and echo our own anxieties . . . and in this way the work, with its unpredictable and disjointed rhythmic violence, reveals itself astonishingly near to us and to our sensibilities as modern men. In any case the second Piano Sonata can be said to have inaugurated a new style of keyboard writing which has since been adopted by other composers in recent years, but which at the time represented a complete break with tradition, as far removed from the innovations of Debussy and Ravel in this field as they were from their ancestors, the great French *clavecinistes* of the seventeenth century.

It was only natural that Boulez should have been for a short time interested in the experiments being carried out in what was then called *musique concrète* in the Paris studios of the French Radio's *Groupe de Recherches* by Pierre Schaeffer (b. 1910) and Pierre Henry (b. 1927); and in 1952 he wrote for them his only essays in this medium which he entitled *Etudes I et II*. It was Schaeffer who first discovered that manipulating and distorting in various ways sounds existing in nature *already recorded* on tape a composer might gain access to a whole new world of 'sounds in the raw' which might prove a valuable extension to the normal musical vocabulary.[1] The theory and procedures on which *musique concrète* is based can be compared to what in film-language is known as 'photo-montage'—that is to say, the artisans of concrete music perform what is really sound-montage. Thus, for example, having recorded the sound of a barrel rolling down an inclined plane, the sounds thus obtained can be manipulated by slowing down, or speeding up, or playing them backwards, or subjecting the tape to any other kind of transformation. The result may then be blended with other sounds—for example the gurgling of escaping bath-water, the bleating of a goat, distorted human voices or machine noises of various kinds—which are then emitted from loudspeakers placed at various points and electrically controlled by the conductor. *Musique concrète* can be effective as background music, or rather 'noises off', in the theatre, but has largely been superseded by electronic music, which differs from concrete in that it is derived from sounds resulting from the manipulation of electric frequencies and vibrations having no connexion with sounds in nature. These vibrations, in fact, do not become audible at all until they leave the loudspeaker or magnetophone; and electronic musicians claim that the sounds they manufacture are unlike any that exist in nature, and are consequently more suitable for abstract composition than those employed by the advocates of concrete music. This may be so, but one of the chief failings of electronic music is the apparently limited range of sounds available, and

[1] For a full and detailed exposition of his theories and methods of composition see: Schaeffer, Pierre: *Traité des objets musicaux*, Paris 1966.

the consequent risk of monotony and lack of colour too often found in such compositions. One of the pioneers of electronic music is the German composer Karlheinz Stockhausen (b. 1928) who, in collaboration with Herbert Eimert, founded the famous Studio of Electronic Music in Cologne. The chief interest to musicians of the electronic experiments now being carried on in Germany, France, Italy and to some extent in England, would appear to be mainly confined to the possibilities they offer of eventually eliminating altogether the interpreter or executant—or, as Boulez has expressed it, of making a synthesis of the human and mechanical elements in performance. The composer is, in fact, his own interpreter; he alone knows what sounds are going to be produced, although he cannot hear them until they issue from the loudspeaker or whatever apparatus is being used. Furthermore, now that music as envisaged by Boulez and his followers is becoming (or, rather, has become) a matter of abstruse calculations dealing almost exclusively with frequencies, pitch, timbre, intensity and extremely subtle experiments in fragmented rhythms which have to be performed with metronomic exactitude, and perhaps at different registers and in different timbres as well, such passages may prove to be unplayable by human agency on any existing form of musical instrument. Here then, is where the electronic musician takes over. His electromagnetic tapes can be cut to fit to the nearest millimetre the exact length of the musical phrase, and can ensure that each metrical fragment, including the silences between the notes, is correctly spaced and timed.

After his single contributions to *musique concrète* in the form of the above-mentioned two Etudes, Boulez soon found himself out of sympathy with the aims of the group and took no further part in their activities, having come to the conclusion that the material with which they were apparently content to work was not really suitable for musical composition, being 'insufficiently malleable and incapable of initiating or sustaining any form of dialectic'.

His next major work, which aroused considerable controversy on account of its uncompromising and rigid formalism, was *Structures I* for two pianos, first performed in 1952 during the Festival held in Paris of *L'Œuvre du XXme siècle*. Here his theories about 'total serialism' are carried to the extreme limits of a purely intellectual exercise, apparently devoid of any normal musical content and consequently inaccessible to the ordinary listener.

In the meantime Boulez was still working with the Madeleine Renaud–Jean-Louis Barrault Company, and in 1954 he founded, under their patronage, the 'Concerts du Petit Marigny' which later became famous as the 'Domaine Musical', a concert-giving association entirely devoted to the promotion of contemporary and mainly avant-garde music. Boulez was by now acquiring an international reputation, and was looked up to everywhere by young progressive musicians as the most significant and dynamic representative of the 'new music' in Europe. His next work, with which his name will always be associated, did perhaps more than any other to consolidate that reputation: it was *Le marteau sans maître* which was performed for the first time under the direction of Hans Rosbaud, at Baden-Baden on 18 June 1955. The work consists of nine pieces, based on three poems by René Char, and is scored for contralto solo, flute, viola, guitar, vibraphone, xylorimba and percussion. It marks a new departure in Boulez' œuvre in so far as, though still constructed basically in accordance with his method, it is tonally far more accessible to the ear and less exclusively cerebral than his previous compositions had been. It has, indeed, a certain sensuous quality, and the scoring for the small orchestra produces sounds that recall here and there the delicate refinements of the Javanese *gamelang*. The spirit of Debussy at times seems not very far away; and it was this new element in a score by Boulez that prompted the German critic Heinrich Strobel to describe the work as 'Webern sounding like Debussy'.

Other key-works in Boulez' later production were *Doubles*

for orchestra (1958) and the third Piano Sonata (1956); but the most important of all the works of his last period, on which he was working for several years, was *Pli selon pli*, a 'Portrait of Mallarmé', incorporating a number of poems treated in a variety of styles and for various instrumental and vocal combinations. In recent years Boulez has shown signs of devoting more and more of his time to conducting, and is now firmly established as one of the outstanding *chefs d'orchestre* of his generation, and internationally very much in demand. He has been appointed titular conductor of the B.B.C. Symphony Orchestra and of the New York Philharmonic as from 1971.

The impact made by Pierre Boulez on the course of contemporary music has had, and is likely to have, far-reaching effects; and his must be reckoned one of the most acute and distinguished musical minds of the century.

It should not, however, be inferred that his rise to prominence in the nineteen-fifties, any more than that of his senior contemporary Olivier Messiaen, were the only significant developments in French music of the period. At least three other composers belonging to the same generation have achieved real distinction in their own different and individual ways: Henri Dutilleux (b. 1916), Maurice Ohana (b. 1914) and Serge Nigg (b. 1924). Three composers whose names are not associated with any particular 'system' or method of composition, but who have been content to develop their own personalities and write, each one, according to his own convictions. It is true that the youngest of the three, Serge Nigg, did at one time experience doubts as to the lines on which modern music ought to develop and what should be the place and function in society of the contemporary composer, and it was his reaction against what he felt was the excessively personal and quasi-mystical idiom of his first teacher Messiaen (whose influence is discernible in his earliest works) that led him to adopt, as an antidote, as it were, to this 'free' style of composition the Schoenbergian serialist technique which gave him the discipline he felt he needed. His first important work in that idiom was the Variations for piano and ten instruments which were included in the programme of the Festival of the International Society for Contemporary Music (I.S.C.M.) at Palermo in 1948. In that same year, however, he underwent another conversion, allowing himself to be influenced by the tendentious Marxist-dictated propaganda of the so-called *Prague Manifesto* calling upon composers to give up being excessively subjective and individualist, and to 'express in their music the sentiments and lofty progressive ideals of the common people'. This was in effect a re-statement of the principles laid down in the notorious 'Ideological Platform of the Russian Association of Proletarian Musicians' of 1929 and in the Zhdanov decrees of 1948 which attempted to impose a musical censorship and caused trouble for composers like Shostakovitch and Prokofiev at that time. This phase in Nigg's career, however, did not last very long, and in the early 'fifties he found and developed a style which was to be characteristically his own; and to this period belong the best of his works, such as the Piano Concerto of 1954 and the Violin Concerto of 1957. Among other works inspired by a literary or pictorial theme may be cited the 'radiophonic ballet' for twelve instruments *L'Etrange aventure de Gulliver à Lilliput* (1958) and the *Jerôme-Bosch Symphonie* (1960) inspired by the famous picture by Hieronymus Bosch in the Prado Museum *The Garden of Delights*.

With Maurice Ohana we are in the presence of a composer of striking originality who has evolved a highly personal style of his own. Of Spanish parentage (Ohana is the name of a village in Andalusia) he was born in Casablanca and gained his first musical impressions from hearing *cantejondo* in southern Spain and Negro and Berber music in North Africa, and nearly all his music is coloured by these memories. Through his long residence in France, which is his country of adoption, Ohana is universally considered to belong to the modern French school with which he has close ties; and it was in Paris that he received the bulk of his musical training. In 1947 he was one of the co-founders of the group *Zodiaque* whose members, including, among others, two young French composers of great promise, Pierre de la Forest Divonne and Alain Bermat, were united in their desire to see music freed from the various doctrinal tyrannies to which, in their view, it had been too long subjected, whether dodecaphonic, Neo-Romantic or 'Progressist'. The group, as such, did not remain long in being, but as a gesture it served its purpose and showed that there were still some independent musical spirits who believed the time had come to 're-humanise' their art. (It is significant that Ohana, unlike the majority of his contemporaries, has never written 'serial' or 'twelve-note' music at any time.)

During the 1945 war Ohana came to England to join the commandos with whom he saw service in many parts of the world, from Scotland to Madagascar; and before settling in Paris he spent some time in Rome where he was in close touch with Alfredo Casella and other members of the young Italian school. His first major work (1950) was a setting of Garcia Lorca's magnificent poem on the death of a famous bull-fighter, Ignacio Sanchez Mejias, who was also a man of letters and a friend of Lorca's and of other Spanish writers. The work is scored for baritone solo, a narrator, a chorus of eight con-tralti in unison and a small orchestra—flute, oboe, two clari-nets, two horns, trumpet, kettle-drums, percussion, harpsi-chord and string quintet; and with an extraordinary economy of means and some highly original sound textures, the com-poser has matched the tragic poem with music that seems to burn and glow at a very high level of intensity.

A feature of Ohana's music is the use he makes of thirds of a tone employing for this purpose a zither specially tuned. The example of the Andalusian *cante jondo*, and indeed, of much Oriental music, is obvious here; but in rationalising this pro-cedure Ohana observes very pertinently: 'The use of these new intervals seems to me to be a natural step towards the conquest of one or more of the harmonics coming next after Debussy's ninths and Ravel's elevenths and thirteenths, etc. The only new thing is that they are deliberately played, and thus enlarge the possibilities of melody to an immense extent.' In his music for the film *Goha* (1957) and the oratorio *Récit de l'an zéro* (1959) Ohana uses the zither tuned in this way to great effect. Besides concertos for the harpsichord and guitar, other notable works by Ohana are the fine *Cantigas* (1954) for chorus and orchestra on old Spanish poems of the twelfth and thirteenth centuries; a *Tombeau de Claude Debussy* (1961) for soprano, piano, zither in thirds of a tone, and chamber orchestra; *Signes* (1965) for flute, piano, zither and percussion; *Synaxis* (1966) for two pianos, four percussion and orchestra; and *Phèdre* (1967) for three actors, two sopranos with harp, zither, harpsichord, piano, four percussion and chamber choir. In 1969 he won the Italia Prize with a work for *a cappella* choir entitled *Cris*.

With a reputation solidly established on the Continent, though unfortunately somewhat less well known in England (though a few works have been broadcast by the B.B.C.), Maurice Ohana undoubtedly adds lustre to the contemporary French musical scene, though the unmistakable Spanish flavour in almost everything he writes should not be under-rated or overlooked. There is here a deep-rooted atavism which accounts for certain tragic, even brutal undertones in his music which, at the same time, like so much in the best Spanish art, contrives to be both visionary and realistic. The idiom is highly personal, and can be uncompromisingly harsh; but nothing is done for effect, and clarity and precision are never sacrificed. There is, in fact, a fundamental purity in this music, both subjective and objective; its inspiration is intuitive and unselfconscious, its realisation highly professional and making no concessions to fashion or spurious aesthetic theories. Above all, it is never divorced from humanity or nature; and in this respect the music of Ohana proclaims its affinity with that of Debussy, Manuel de Falla, his old master, and Erik Satie, certain of whose works, in the words of Ohana, 'situated outside time and, in a sense, outside the space of his particular epoch, seem to represent a clearing in the forest of art where aesthetic theories are forgotten and where music alone is present without any reference whatsoever to its creator'. Acutely conscious of the problem confronting composers today, Ohana believes that 'the deep meaning of contemporary language is still to be discovered', and in each new work he strives, with complete integrity, to evolve a mode of speech which will not only reflect the quality of his own musical thinking but be in harmony with the spirit of the age.

Another notable representative of contemporary French music who pursues an independent path is Henri Dutilleux. A strong sense of style and a preoccupation with form lend his music a distinction which is highly civilised but does not in any way hamper the free expression of a temperament in which order and fantasy are nicely balanced. He was awarded the Grand Prix de Rome for composition on the eve of the war, but it was only after 1945 that, like so many of his contemporaries, he felt the time had come, if not to abandon, at least to renovate the traditional language of music, and solved this problem, not by adhering to any 'school' or 'system' but by forging for himself a highly personal idiom, in no way revolutionary, but distinctive. And thus the production of his first Symphony in 1951, at a time when few composers were writing symphonies, was not only a land-mark in post-war French music but a personal triumph that established him as one of the leading composers of his generation. Dutilleux has never sought the limelight, and his output to date has been restricted to a relatively small number of works of high quality.[1] The work that first brought him into the public eye was the ballet *Le Loup* produced by Roland Petit in 1953 on a scenario by Anouilh with memorable scenery by Carzou, for which he wrote the music. The ballet had a great success in which Dutilleux's music played an important part. The following year Charles Münch conducted the first symphony in

---

[1] Notably, besides the symphonies and ballets, a remarkable Piano Sonata (1948), a setting for baritone and orchestra of *Trois Sonnets de Jean Cassou* (1954), and *Cinq métaboles* for orchestra (1966).

Boston and New York, and the work made such an impression that the composer was commissioned by Münch and the Kussevitzky Foundation to write a second symphony which had its *première* in Boston in 1959. The following year Münch introduced it in France at the Besançon Festival where it was enthusiastically received by critics and public alike. In the words of one well-known critic[1]: 'The architectural and orchestral structure here disappears behind the inspiration of the artist and poet who, in the course of the work's three movements, evokes for us dream worlds that are by turn mysterious and vehement. The music has the same fairy-like yet anguished atmosphere of *Le Grand Meaulnes*[2]; it reflects, too, the musical obsessions of our age in the subtle organisation of its rhythmic and thematic material and in the spatial pointillism of its orchestration. . . .'

An almost exact contemporary of Dutilleux and, like him, a composer of high principles who all his life has been a fervent 'independent', is Marcel Landowski (b. 1915) who has the distinction of having composed four operas at a time when few of his contemporaries were interested in this form; they are *Le Fou, Le Ventriloque, Les Adieux* and *L'Opéra de poussière*, all composed between 1956 and 1962. A firm believer in both liberty and tradition, he is neither an extremist nor a reactionary, and occupies today an important post in the Ministry of Cultural Affairs.

Another completely undogmatic composer who has been a force in contemporary French music is Henry Barraud (b. 1900) who for many years presided over the music department of the French Radio. Suspicious of a great deal of the so-called 'new' music, Barraud has never concealed his distrust of innovation for the sake of innovation or the cult of specialised procedures and techniques masking an absence of genuine musical feeling and invention. Like Koechlin, he has always attached great importance to a genuine melodic line; and, although he has

---

[1] Claude Rostand in *Le Monde*.
[2] The famous novel by Alain Fournier published in 1913.

sometimes utilised, as for example in his third symphony, various systems in vogue—atonal, polytonal and even serial—his music remains basically diatonic and has the serenity and stability associated with Gregorian plainsong. It was Barraud, indeed, who once declared that Gregorian chant is the folklore of France. In addition to three symphonies, he has written chamber music, a piano concerto, a cantata on the *Testament de Villon* and a grand opera, on a libretto by Salvador de Madariaga, *Numance*. As Director of music on the French Radio he invariably maintained high standards and was always willing to encourage genuine talent among young composers. Unfortunately during the last years of the Gaullist regime French broadcasting and television became little more than a mouthpiece of the Government, and even the cultural channels were adversely affected—so much so that at one time the decree went forth that there would be no place for contemporary music in the programmes. The situation may be slightly better today, but there is little official encouragement for the young composer.

Up to now in this chapter we have been dealing almost exclusively with composers of relative maturity who have made a name for themselves since the second world war and are now generally considered to represent the most recent trends in modern French music. There are, however, many younger men now coming to the fore, and although it would clearly be premature to attempt to pass any kind of judgment on their work at this stage, it would be unjust not to mention at least a few names of those of the present generation who have already shown, not only promise, but achievement. If serialism today is dead, other forms of experimental techniques are very much alive. Some composers have recourse to computers, others to electronic gadgets while others again write what is called 'aleatory' or 'indeterminate' music, preferring to leave at least some proportion of their work to chance or to the improvisatory inspiration of the performer. Works written for percussion instruments alone were much in favour in the late 'sixties, and composers found in the fine Strasbourg Percussion Ensemble, using an immense range of instruments with a high degree of virtuosity, the ideal interpreters of works of this kind.

Among composers of the younger generation one of the best known is Gilbert Amy (b. 1936) who succeeded Boulez as director of the *Domaine musical* organisation for the promotion of new music; while André Boucourechliev (b. 1925) and Jean Barraqué (b. 1928) have both written large-scale works in an advanced idiom, making use of magnetophones and mechanically produced sounds as well as conventional instruments. The Greek-born Yannis Xenakis (b. 1922) writes partly computerised music, and has shown himself to be a manipulator of sound effects of sometimes startling originality and ingeniously contrived, though their connexion with music is not always apparent.

Among present-day French composers of less extreme tendencies whose reputation stands high today, and who have done work of distinction and importance, are Claude Balliff (b. 1924), Maurice Le Roux (b. 1923), Maurice Jarre (b. 1924) and Marius Constant (b. 1925). Balliff is both composer and theoretician, an independent belonging to no 'school'; Le Roux, a one-time pupil of Messiaen, writes his own, very personal kind of serial music, and is known also as conductor, critic, musicologist and lecturer on the history of music in schools; Jarre has specialised in music for the theatre and has been closely associated with the *Théâtre National Populaire* (T.N.P.); and Constant, who studied with both Enesco and Messiaen, has written, besides ballet scores and music destined for the radio, symphonic music of considerable distinction, notably the *Préludes* for orchestra, and an important symphonic suite composed in homage to *Turner*.

Constant has also experimented with so-called 'aleatory' music (derived from the Latin *alea*, a game played with dice) of which Stockhausen in Germany and Xenakis in France are the principal exponents today; and in one of his more recent works he employs a dancer instead of a conductor whose gyrations, inspired by the reading by an actor on the platform of a text by Lautréamont, are supposed to give the players their cue and help them to decide which notes, among alternatives supplied by the composer, they should play at any given moment.

Another word employed to indicate the element of Chance in musical composition (this time derived from the Greek) is 'stochastic', a purely mathematical term used in connexion with the law of great numbers used in calculating probabilities. It is associated more especially with the works of Xenakis who came to music *via* architecture and mathematics and, as already indicated above, sometimes works in collaboration with an electronic computer.[1]

At a time when so much of the music being written today is of so patently an experimental character, it would be both profitless and out of place to attempt even a relative assessment of merit and accomplishment among the young composers who are representing France today; and any such estimates can safely be left to posterity. My object in these pages has been to trace an outline of the trends and tendencies that have marked the evolution of French music during the present century and to give some account of the leading personalities who have contributed most to securing for it the prestige it now enjoys.

To complete this survey there follows now a review of some of the specific forms in which French music throughout the century has manifested itself: in opera, ballet and 'places where they sing.'

[1] For a detailed analysis of the methods employed by Xenakis the reader is referred to an excellent publication dealing with various aspects of contemporary music by Henry Barraud: *Pour comprendre les musiques d'aujourd'hui* (with numerous musical examples on disk), Paris 1968.

CHAPTER TEN

I. DEVELOPMENTS IN OPERA

II. BALLET

III. CHORAL MUSIC

I

During the three centuries that separate *Pelléas et Mélisande* from Monteverdi's *Orfeo*, opera in France had undergone many transformations. The most radical changes occurred in the nineteenth century when opera for the first time became accessible to a far wider public than in the days when Lully in the seventeenth, and Rameau in the eighteenth, along with a host of other minor Court composers, were producing their works for the exclusive delectation of a very small aristocratic intelligentsia, and depended for their livelihood almost entirely on Royal patronage. They were essentially musicians of the Establishment, and operated in a world to which the ordinary public virtually had no access. Nor, it must be added, would the ordinary public of those days have been sufficiently educated to appreciate such entertainment even if it had come their way. This 'closed circuit' atmosphere in the arts, however, was gradually dissipated after the French Revolution at the end of the eighteenth century, and in the early years of the nineteenth artists and composers had to satisfy other and wider tastes.

There is no doubt that the maxims laid down by Gluck in the middle of the eighteenth century for the reform of opera (in his preface to *Alceste* in 1767) had a great influence; and from that moment it could be said that the foundations of modern 'expressive', or naturalistic opera were laid. Indeed, it is clear that Wagner merely built on Gluck's foundations, broadly speaking, when he created his own particular brand of

Music Drama. (The 'Leitmotif', however, was his own invention introduced in order to preserve a certain unity, and to set
up fixed points here and there in the freely flowing current of
declamation, supported by an ever-changing and flexible
orchestral mass which was what Wagner substituted for the
old sequences of formal recitatives and arias.)

The position of Mozart in the hierarchy of operatic composers is peculiar and, in a sense, unique. Outwardly a Mozart
opera is composed of recitatives and arias and ensembles on
the model of Paisiello or Cimarosa or any of his Italian contemporaries; but instead of being lay-figures, Mozart's per-
sonages live, and character is infused into them in a miraculous
way through the music allotted to them to sing. It is probable
that Mozart, who was forty years junior to Gluck, had studied
his operas and was aware of his principles; but what he
achieved in opera is so outstanding that it cannot be attributed
to the influence of any other composer or theorist, but solely
to Mozart's own infallible intuition and perspicacity in all
matters pertaining to his art. And so, at one stroke, Mozart
created the perfect opera where the claims of theatrical convention and of human nature are blended as never before or
since, and where the divinest of music is poured into moulds
which may have been cast by tradition, but which, in Mozart's
hands, offer no suggestion of artificiality or constraint.

But despite all the progress that had been achieved in
Western Europe, Italian opera still pursued its old course more
or less unchanged, and unaffected by Gluck's reforms, reach-
ing its high watermark with the uncontestably great productions of Verdi, and continuing with Puccini and such masters
of 'verismo' as Mascagni and Leoncavallo. Nevertheless,
speaking generally, nineteenth-century Italian opera was still
conceived of as being primarily a vehicle for vocal acrobatics,
scant attention being paid to the claims of either naturalism or
artistic or dramatic propriety of any kind. Nonsensical libretti
were no obstacle to the purveyors of conventional opera of
this kind, nor did their public expect or care about anything

better than what they habitually got so long as their favourite tenor or soprano was provided with the right sort of material to sing—and sang it to perfection.

The purely sensuous appeal of the singing voice has always exercised a peculiar attraction over Southern Latins, which accounts for the great popularity of opera in Italy, and especially of the kind of opera where more stress is laid on the emotional and spectacular than on the intellectual or purely aesthetic aspects of the drama; it is not therefore surprising that operatic music is so often apt to be both trivial and insincere.

In France in the nineteenth century very much the same ideals prevailed until, there too, eventually the influence of Wagner began to make itself felt, not always with the happiest results. Until that happened, however, French operatic composers had tended to cultivate the smaller and lighter forms of opera, ranging from the specifically French *opéra-comique* to operetta—a form which Saint-Saëns, in one of his *bons mots*, once described as 'the daughter of the opéra-comique—a daughter who went to the bad. Not that daughters who go to the bad', he added, 'are always lacking in charm.'[1] And thus it came about that during the first half at least of the nineteenth century in France it was these two forms of operatic entertainment that dominated the scene; and the composers who became famous in this field, many of them extremely gifted and highly competent musicians, were men like Auber, Boïeldieu, Grétry, Hérold, Monsigny, Dalayrac, Philidor, Thomas, Offenbach, Adam and Lecoq. The only real purveyor of 'grand opera' at its grandest at this period was Meyerbeer; and he was not a Frenchman but a German Jew whom Rossini had encouraged to try his fortune in France. In a class apart, meanwhile, were two outstanding French composers, Charles Gounod and Georges Bizet, whose names will always be indissolubly linked with the two most famous operas in the world—*Faust* and *Carmen*. Nor must we forget their illustrious predecessor Hector Berlioz who can also claim to have made

[1] Quoted by Martin Cooper in *Opéra Comique*, London, (1949).

history with certain of his stage-works, though with none of these did he ever achieve the kind of popularity that have made *Faust* and *Carmen* household words in almost every corner of the globe.

This, then, was roughly the situation as regards opera in France when the twentieth century dawned. And only two years after it had dawned an event took place which was to have far-reaching effects on the future of opera as an art-form. This was, of course, the production in the spring of 1902 of Debussy's *Pelléas et Mélisande*, a masterpiece which stands alone among operas, so different is it from anything that preceded it, and so pregnant with possibilities for the future—possibilities which have not been lost on twentieth-century composers. *Pelléas*, in fact, was based on an entirely new aesthetic: some have seen in it traces of Wagnerian influence—of Wagner upside-down, as it were—while others connect it with Mussorgsky; but in the last resort it defies classification, except in so far as it can be considered as a prototype in itself. In *Pelléas* Debussy carried the subordination of music to the drama to greater lengths than had ever before been attempted; yet at the same time the whole work is bathed in an atmosphere which is quintessentially musical. Here are no opportunities for displays of vocal virtuosity, no melodramatic 'scenes'; but the poignancy of the drama, all interior, is enhanced a thousandfold by the subtlest and most unobtrusive means. *Pelléas*, then, is a landmark in the history of opera, marking a new orientation in the development of lyric drama, in the same way that the early Florentine operas and those of Monteverdi were landmarks, and later those of Gluck and his school which led, through Mozart and Weber, to Wagner, and so to what we call 'modern' opera.

The attitude of twentieth-century composers towards this particular art-form has been dictated partly by aesthetic, partly by economic considerations. One fact stands out, and that is that there has been, on the whole, a definite trend away from opera in which many contemporary composers can see no future, looking upon it as an outmoded form—which indeed, in many ways it is. At the same time, the enormous cost of producing an opera in the times in which we live acts as a deterrent to composers who might otherwise be tempted to experiment in this direction, since they know only too well that the chances of ever seeing their work produced are so slender as to be almost non-existent. The impact of two wars had also caused, not only economic, but social and artistic upheavals which have not been propitious for new developments in opera, though there have been of course, in the last sixty years, isolated experiments like *Wozzeck*, for example, which have made their mark.

In France nevertheless, where the tradition of the 'lyric theatre' is still strong and opera-going not yet an altogether extinct pastime, there have been perhaps more operas produced during the present century than in any other European country; and the following selective (but by no means exhaustive) list will give some idea of what the operatic output has been in that country and the number of composers of all schools who have contributed to it.

Some operas (including opéra-comique and opéra-bouffe)
produced in France between 1900 and the present day

(All dates are dates of production)

AUBERT, Louis	*La forêt bleue* (1913)
BARRAUD, Henry	*Numance* (1950)
BEYDTS, Louis	*Moineau* (operetta), *Canards Mandarins*, *La SADMP* (opéra-bouffe, lib. Sacha Guitry) (1913)
BONDEVILLE, Emmanuel de	*L'Ecole des maris* (1935)
BRÉVILLE, Pierre de	*Eros vainqueur* (1910)

BRUNEAU, Alfred	*L'Ouragan* (1901), *L'Enfant-Roi* (1905), *Les quatre journées* (1916) (all lib. by Zola); *Le Roi Candaule* (1920), *Le jardin du Paradis* (1923), *Angelo* (1928), *Virginie* (1931). (*Le Rêve* and *L'Attaque du moulin* were both produced before 1900)
BÜSSER, Henri	*Colomba* (1921), *Les noces Corinthiennes* (1922), *La Pie borgne* (1929), *Le Carrosse du Saint-Sacrement*
CAPDEVIELLE, Pierre	*Les amants captifs* (1950)
CHARPENTIER, Gustave	*Louise* (1900), *Julien* (1913)
DEBUSSY	*Pelléas et Mélisande* (1902)
DELANNOY, Marcel	*Le Poirier de misère* (1904), *Philippine* (operetta), *Ginévra* (1942), *Puck* (after Shakespeare) (1946)
DELVINCOURT, Claude	*La femme à barbe* (op. bouffe) (1938), *Lucifer* (a 'mystery') (1949)
DÉODAT de SÉVÉRAC	*Le cœur du moulin* (1909)
DUKAS, Paul	*Ariane et Barbe-Bleue* (1907)
DUPONT, Gabriel	*La Cabrera* (1904), *La farce du cuvier* (1912), *La Glu* (1910), *Antar* (1921)
FAURÉ, Gabriel	*Prométhée* (1900), *Pénélope* (1913)
FÉVRIER, Henri	*Le Roi aveugle* (1906), *Monna Vanna* (1909), *Agnès, dame galante* (1912), *Carmosine* (1913), *Gismonda* (1919), *La damnation de Blanchefleur* (1920), *La femme nue* (1920), *Sylvette* (1932)
GROVLEZ, Gabriel	*Psyché* (1922), *Cœur de rubis* (1922), *Le Marquis de Carabas* (op. bouffe) (1936)
GUY-ROPARTZ, Joseph	*Le Pays* (1913)
HAHN, Reynaldo	*La Carmélite* (1902), *Nausicaa* (op. comique, 1919), *La Ciboulette* (operetta, 1923), *Marchand de Venise* (1935)

HONEGGER, Arthur	4 operas: *Judith* (1926), *Antigone* (1927), *L'Aiglon* (1937), *Charles le Téméraire* (1944) 2 operettas: *Les aventures du Roi Pausole* (1930), *Les petites Cardinal* (1937) 1 melodrama: *Amphion* (1931)
HÜE, Georges	*Le Roi de Paris* (1910), *Titania* (1903), *Le miracle* (1910), *Dans l'ombre de la Cathédrale* (1921), *Riquet à la houppe* (1928)
HURÉ, Jean	*Le bois sacré* (op. comique)
IBERT, Jacques	*Angélique* (1927), *On ne saurait penser à tout* (1928), *Persée et Andromède* (Jules Laforgue) (1929), *Le Roi d'Yvetot* (1930), *Gonzague* (1935), *L'Aiglon* (1937), *La famille Cardinal* (1938)
D'INDY, Vincent	*L'Etranger* (1903), *La légende de Saint Christophe* (1920), *Le rêve de Cinyras* (1927) (*Fervaal* was produced prior to 1900)
JAUBERT, Maurice	*Contrebande* (1929), *Barbe-Bleue* (opéra-minute) (1935)
JOLIVET, André	*Dolores, ou le miracle de la femme laide* (1942)
KOECHLIN, Charles	*Jacob et Laban* (1908—prod. 1925)
LADMIRAULT, Paul	*Myrdhin* (1902)
LANDOWSKI, Marcel	*Le Fou* (1956), *Le ventriloque* (1957), *Les Adieux* (1960), *L'Opéra de poussière* (1962)
LAZZARI, Sylvio	*La Tour de feu* (1928), *La Lépreuse* (1912), *Le Sautériot* (1920), *Melaenis* (1927)

MAGNARD, Alberic — *Bérénice* (1911), *Guercœur* (1931) (reconstructed posthumously by Guy-Ropartz)

MARTELLI, Henri — *La Chanson de Roland* (1923)

MARTINON, Jean — *Hécube* (1953)

MASSENET, Jules — *Grisélidis* (1901), *Le Jongleur de Notre Dame* (1902), *Marie-Magdeleine* (orig. an oratorio) (1903), *Chérubin* (1905), *Ariane* (1906), *Thérèse* (1907), *Bacchus* (1909), *Don Quichotte* (1910), *Roma* (1912), *Panurge* (posth. 1913), *Cléopâtre* (posth. 1914), *Amadis* (posth. 1922)

MESSAGER, André — *Les Dragons de l'Impératrice* (1905), *Fortunio* (1907), *Béatrice* (1914), *Monsieure Beaucaire* (Birmingham, 1919), *La petite fonctionnaire* (1921), *L'Amour masqué* (1923), *Passionnément* (1926), *Coup de roulis* (posth. 1930). All operettas

MILHAUD, Darius — 8 operas: *La brebis égarée* (1923), *Les malheurs d'Orphée* (1926), *Le pauvre matelot* (1927), *Christophe Colomb* (Berlin, 1930), *Maximilien* (1932), *Esther de Carpentras* (1938), *Bolivar* (1943), *David* (1954)
1 one-act: *Médée* (1939)
3 'opéra-minutes': *L'Enlèvement d'Europe*, *L'Abandon d'Ariane*, *La Délivrance de Thésée* (prod. Germany 1927–8)

PIERNÉ, Gabriel — *La fille de Tabarin* (1901), *La coupe enchantée* (1905), *On ne badine pas avec l'amour* (1910), *Sophie Arnould* (1927)

POULENC, Francis	*Les mamelles de Tirésias* (1944), *Dialogues des Carmélites* (1957), *La voix humaine* (1958)
RABAUD, Henri	*La fille de Roland* (1904), *Marouf* (1914), *L'Appel de la mer* (based on Synge's *Riders to the sea*) (1924), *Rolande et le mauvais garçon* (1934)
RAVEL, Maurice	*L'Heure espagnole* (1911), *L'Enfant et les Sortilèges* (1925)
ROGER-DUCASSE, Jean-Jules	*Cantegril* (1931)
ROLAND-MANUEL, Alexis	*Isabelle et Pantalon* (op. bouffe) (1922), *Le Diable amoureux* (1929)
ROUSSEL, Albert	*Padmâvati* (1923) (opera-ballet), *La naissance de la lyre* (1925), *Le testament de la tante Caroline* (1937) (op. bouffe)
SAINT-SAËNS, Camille	*Les barbares* (1901), *Hélène* (1904), *L'Ancêtre* (1906), *Déjanire* (1911)
SAMUEL-ROUSSEAU, Marc	*Tarass-Boulba* (1919), *Le Hulla* (1923), *Le bon Roi Dagobert* (1927)
SAUGUET, Henri	*Le plumet du Colonel* (op. bouffe) (1924), *Un amour du Titien* (operetta) (1928), *La contrebasse* (op. bouffe) (1930), *La Chartreuse de Parme* (1939), *La gageure imprévue* (1944)
TAILLEFERRE, Germaine	*Le marin du Bolivar* (op. bouffe) (1937)
TOMASI, Henri	*L'Atlantide* (1954), *Le triomphe de Jeanne, Il Poverello*

Perhaps the most significant fact to be revealed by this table is that very few operas have been produced in France since world war II, and only two since 1960. Neither Boulez nor Messiaen have written for the stage, and scarcely any of the younger generation formed in their school have tried their hand at opera. The composer of today is more inclined to write for ballet, or incidental music to accompany some stage spectacle; others, again, confine themselves to films. Even the mini-opera seems no longer to be in favour; the accent in modern music today is on the abstract rather than the pictorial, and the style of writing for the voice in vogue today, doing violence to, rather than respecting its natural inflexions, is anything but operatic in the accepted sense of the term.

Moreover, it is not only to opera, but to all forms of vocal writing that these considerations apply today. It is no exaggeration to say that present-day methods of writing for the voice have completely revolutionised vocal techniques. While it is true of course that harmonic emancipation and the tendency to think 'vertically' instead of 'horizontally' has resulted inevitably in a sacrifice of what used to be called 'melody', the new style of vocal writing is not entirely due to harmonic considerations. It corresponds essentially to that desire to increase the *expressive* powers of music which is the real motive force behind all recent innovations in musical techniques. And as the human voice is generally considered to be an 'expressive' instrument *par excellence*, modern composers have naturally endeavoured to enlarge its expressive powers as much as possible. In many cases this has been done, paradoxically enough as it may seem at first sight, by 'demusicalising' the voice, i.e., by insisting upon its essential nature as an organ, not of song, but of speech. Thus the characteristic of much vocal writing during the last century, from Mussorgsky, through Debussy and modern French composers down to Schoenberg and Stravinsky and beyond, has been the tendency to discourage pure singing, and to make the voice part of a kind of rhythmic recitation. On the one hand this practice may be considered a simple reaction against the conventional florid vocal style of former epochs, when the sense of the words was frequently lost sight of under a mass of irrelevant ornament, and accents were ruthlessly displaced or ignored altogether. But it is also the natural result of an increasing interest in, and preoccupation with, literature on the part of modern musicians, and of a desire to be scrupulously faithful to the author's text. The introduction of *vers libre* also allowed for a corresponding relaxation of form in musical settings, and prose is now frequently 'set'. Notable examples are the *Histoires naturelles* of Ravel, or Satie's *Socrate*—both interesting examples of the modern style of writing for the voice.

A still more radical example of the revolt against, not only melody, but the maintenance of even a singing 'tone' is to be found in the experiments that have been carried out in that hybrid form of vocal declamation known as 'Sprechmelodie' or 'Sprechgesang' of which one of the best known examples is to be found in Schoenberg's *Pierrot Lunaire* (1910). Here the part written for the voice has to be transformed into a 'spoken melody', while at the same time the performer must adhere strictly to the written notes. The difference between a 'sung note' and a 'spoken note' is that whereas the former is held by the voice, the latter is merely indicated, and then abandoned in either an upward or downward direction. And yet Schoenberg expressly indicates that the singer must avoid any form of expression resembling either declamation or singing proper, so that the effect in performance is (or should be) that of a speaking voice which, though avoiding definitely musical notes, is yet observant of pitch and rhythm. The performer, in fact, must aim at producing a 'speaking tone' ('Sprechton') midway between singing proper ('Gesangston') and declamation. The musical notes must nevertheless be indicated and the exact intervals observed, but in a 'speaking' voice almost completely devoid of tone.

This is an innovation in vocal technique which has had a considerable influence on contemporary methods of writing for the voice; and in a great many modern scores it is carried to sometimes violent and even ludicrous extremes. One result has been that great demands are made on the technical virtuosity of singers who specialise in music of this kind, often written in an extremely disjointed style and characterised by wide leaps from the highest to the lowest notes in the singer's vocal compass, and little or nothing in the way of a sustained melodic line. In France, as elsewhere, this style of vocal writing is favoured by contemporary composers, and many examples can be found in the works of Boulez and Messiaen among others.

All this would suggest that there is little prospect of an operatic revival in France today, where the trend is definitely away from what is now generally considered to be an obsolete and irrelevant art-form incapable of reflecting the mood and spirit of the age.

As with most other musical activities, opera is more or less confined to Paris and to one or other of the State-controlled establishments, the *Opéra* and the *Opéra-Comique*. In the provinces, Nice, Monte-Carlo, Toulouse and Bordeaux have opera-houses where productions of new works occasionally take place; and the *Théâtre des Champs-Elysées* in Paris is often used for visiting companies or special productions of works not in the official repertory. New works are also sometimes tried out at some of the annual music festival centres, such as Aix-en-Provence, Bordeaux or Strasbourg.

II

As if to compensate for the comparative lack of interest in opera shown by late twentieth-century composers, there has been in the course of the century a marked revival of interest in the ballet as an art-form. This was especially noticeable in the twenty years between the first appearance in Paris in 1909 of Serge Diaghilev and his famous *Ballets Russes* and his death in 1929; and the interest which is being taken today in ballet in all its forms by present-day musicians is undoubtedly due to the enormous and far-reaching influence of Diaghilev, whose principal contribution was the achievement of a synthesis of the arts of music, painting and dancing such as had never been seen before. The Russian Ballet, in fact, summed up and epitomised in a most remarkable way the aesthetic and social tendencies and beliefs of a whole generation; and from 1909 to 1929 it was a unique and inimitable artistic entity which owed its supremacy to the extraordinary personality of its creator who was able to group round him and hold together an unrivalled company of collaborators—not only the finest dancers in the world, but a great many of the leading artists and composers of the day.

From a strictly musical point of view, the list of masterpieces which owe their existence entirely to the Russian Ballet of Diaghilev is an imposing one. Stravinsky alone contributed eight scores which are landmarks in modern music; and in France, from Debussy and Ravel downwards, there were few composers who were not directly or indirectly inspired to write ballets either at that time or later. Debussy's *Jeux* commissioned by Diaghilev may not have been a success as a ballet, but today it is universally acknowledged to be a masterpiece of symphonic writing, and one of the key works in the whole contemporary movement. Ravel's *Daphnis et Chloë* is also outstanding in twentieth-century symphonic music and, like *Jeux*, can be considered as a piece of 'pure' music, quite independent of scenic presentation. Other notable French ballets called into being by Diaghilev, were Poulenc's *Les Biches*, Sauguet's *La Chatte*, and three by Georges Auric: *Les Fâcheux*, *Les Matelots* and *Pastorale*. Milhaud contributed *Le Train Bleu* on a rather trivial scenario by Cocteau; but his best ballets, *La création du monde* and *L'Homme et son désir* were commissioned and produced by Rolf de Mare's Swedish Ballet company which was specialising in avant-garde productions at that time. Among other ballets by Milhaud are *Salade*, an essay in the style of the Italian *Commedia dell'Arte* in a modern idiom, a ballet on the theme of E. A. Poe's *The Bells* (Chicago, 1946) and one that he composed for Roland Petit in 1948 entitled *'adame Miroir*.

Honegger, too, wrote music for several ballets, but not for Diaghilev; of these *Skating Rink* (1922) is perhaps the best known. He also wrote during the nineteenth-thirties two ballets, *Sémiramis* and *Un oiseau blanc s'est envolé*, on scenarios by Paul Valéry and Sacha Guitry respectively.

Composers of an older school, like Dukas and Roussel, also wrote distinguished ballet scores; and mention has already been made in these pages of the former's *poème dansé*, *La Péri* (1912), and the two Roussel ballets *Bacchus et Ariane* and *Aeneas*, both produced in the nineteen-thirties.

This is not the place for a catalogue of notable French ballets; it has merely been my intention to show that in France, as elsewhere, ballet, as distinct from opera, has been a stimulating influence upon modern composers. There are many reasons for this; one is that in the post-war world of haste and stress 'grand' opera, at least, is felt to be something of an anachronism in comparison with ballet which not only moves more swiftly but allows the composer unlimited scope to express in his music all the implications, both hidden and apparent, suggested by a given situation, instead of having to limit himself, as in opera, to the expression of the particular one defined by words put into the singers' mouth. Ballet, in fact, being mute is more suggestive; and it is this quality of being able to convey emotion through suggestion which is the special prerogative of ballet, that may explain why modern composers are writing more ballets than operas. For example, the scene in *Petruchka* where the Moor is trying to defeat his *ennui* by idly playing with a coconut, while in the orchestra two themes that won't fit pursue each other indolently, is charged with an inexpressible emotion which no spoken words could possibly suggest; while the climax of the same ballet, when the magician has shown the people that Petruchka was only a doll, and his ghost suddenly appears over the top of the booth, gesticulating through the snowflakes, seems to open a door on to the infinite.

It is in such scenes as these that the peculiar magic of ballet at its best is most apparent. Both ballet and opera are governed very largely by theatrical convention, but in so far as ballet shows less desire to compromise with real life than opera, it may therefore be—though some might dispute this—a purer form of art. For, while operatic convention does not exclude a degree of realism which may be ludicrous and is often irksome, ballet moves in a stylised world of its own where fantasy, rather than realism, reigns supreme. At the same time, it obviously has its limitations, not least of which, as devotees of opera will not fail to point out, is that in it there is no place for the human singing voice that gives to opera its unquestionable hold upon the public's affections. Furthermore it is undoubtedly true that more great music of enduring quality has been immortalised in opera than has ever been, or is likely to be, inspired by ballet. It may well be, indeed, that opera is only suffering a temporary eclipse, and ballet enjoying only a temporary vogue; all the chronicler can do is to report on trends as he observes them, and leave it to others to draw their own conclusions.

III

Whereas in most European countries communal singing is felt to be a natural form of expression, and in rural as well as in urban districts is looked upon as an agreeable recreation and of all forms of music-making the most accessible and the least exacting, choral music in France has never been widely cultivated or indulged in by the masses as a form of relaxation or distraction. On a more sophisticated level, however, as a recognised art-form with both secular and religious associations, it has never been neglected, and throughout the centuries a fine tradition of choral singing has been established which has lasted more or less until the present day. In the mid-nineteenth century choral music had come to mean, broadly speaking, church music, typical examples of which can be found in the oratorios and cantatas on religious themes by Charles Gounod and César Franck. Then in 1888 Fauré composed his now famous *Requiem* in memory of his father, and in the following year Alfred Bruneau, better known as an operatic composer, produced a remarkable full-scale Requiem Mass which deserves to be better known. (It was performed by the Bach Choir in London, under the direction of Sir Charles Stanford, in 1896.)

During the next half-century choral music as such was somewhat neglected, and religious music also, until new life was breathed into a genre which had inevitably suffered an eclipse by Francis Poulenc, notably in his Gloria, Stabat Mater and *Sept Répons des Ténèbres*. The decline in choral music was largely due to the reaction that had set in against Italian-style opera and to the growing tendency among modern composers to treat the voice as an instrument more for supplying a particular tone-colour than as a vehicle for lyrical effusions or virtuoso display. Hence the practice of adding a wordless chorus to symphonic works such as we find, e.g., in *Sirènes* (the third of Debussy's Nocturnes), in Ravel's ballet *Daphnis et Chloë* and in the Evocations of Albert Roussel. Nevertheless, there are at least two major choral works of this period: Roussel's setting (to English words) of *Psalm 80*, and Florent Schmitt's of *Psalm 47*. Schmitt also composed for the Paris Exhibition of 1937 his *Fete de la Lumière* for soprano, chorus and orchestra, as well as some half-dozen *a cappella* works written between 1896 and 1943.

Charles Koechlin also made an important contribution to choral music in the early part of the century; and whereas until now the style of choral writing had been more or less in line with the classical or late Romantic tradition, Koechlin introduced a new element by drawing freely on two hitherto little used sources—Gregorian chant and folk-song. The modal character of much of his music is one of its great charms, and is nowhere more effective than in his big cantata for solo voice, chorus, organ and orchestra *L'Abbaye*. The work is in two parts: the first was composed between 1899 and 1902, and the second between 1906 and 1908. Other notable choral works by Koechlin are the choruses in his *Trois poèmes du Livre de la*

Jungle (1899–1910) and the *Chant funèbre à la mémoire de jeunes femmes défuntes* (1902–7) for double chorus, organ and orchestra.

The revival of interest in folk-music in France was largely due to the work of Louis Bourgault-Ducoudray (1840–1910) in the late nineteenth century, whose modal harmonisations of folk-tunes of different countries, including Greece, Brittany, Scotland and Wales are models of their kind. Other composers who, following the lead thus given by the scholarly Bourgault-Ducoudray, helped to enrich the repertory of choral societies and singers throughout France by bringing to light a considerable body of hitherto unknown regional folk-music, were Maurice Emmanuel (1862–1938) for Burgundian songs, Vincent d'Indy for the folk music of the Cévennes, and Charles Bordes (1863–1909) in his harmonisation of folk-tunes of the Basque countries. Gradually a whole new school of 'regional' composers came into being, notably, for Brittany: Paul Ladmirault (1877–1944), Jean Huré (1877–1930) and Guy-Ropartz (1864–1955); for the Auvergne: Joseph Canteloube (1879–1957); and for Provence: Déodat de Sévérac (1873–1921).

Although neither Debussy nor Ravel left any major purely choral works, yet they both showed an extraordinary mastery of the medium whenever they attempted it. One has only to think of the skilful and imaginative handling of voices in such things as the choruses in *Le Martyre de St. Sébastien*, or even in *La Damoiselle élue*; the delightful unaccompanied *Trois chansons de Charles d'Orléans* and the female chorus in *Sirènes,* to feel that all these examples seem perfectly to fulfil Debussy's own ideal of a 'a style of choral writing which is extremely simple but also extremely flexible'. Ravel, too, wrote impeccably for the voice, though apart from the wordless chorus in *Daphnis et Chloë* and the *Trois Chansons* for mixed *a cappella* choir there are no purely choral works in his *œuvre*.

Among composers of an older generation, one who has perhaps produced more in this field than any other is Georges

Migot (see Chapter 8) whose large output has been principally in the form of large-scale cantatas, oratorios and other works for choral ensembles of various kinds. These include a complete cycle of spiritual oratorios on the life of Christ (*The Annunciation, The Nativity of Our Lord, The Sermon on the Mount, The Passion, The Entombment* and *The Resurrection*) all composed between 1936 and 1954, and another oratorio *Saint Germain d'Auxerre* described as a *chanson de geste* for three mixed choirs and soloists, unaccompanied. Migot has also written a *Requiem* for chorus *a cappella*.

Most of the works already mentioned have been, by and large, firmly fixed in the French tradition. It was left to three members of the group of 'Les Six'—Honegger, Milhaud and Poulenc, to introduce in their choral compositions a new, more revolutionary style of writing for the human voice. In Milhaud's incidental music to Claudel's adaptation of the *Oresteia* of Aeschylus (*Agamemnon, Les Choéphores* and *Les Euménides*) composed between 1913 and 1922, there are passages where the chorus is directed to shriek and shout and whistle, and much of the vocal writing consists largely of pitchless declamation. Milhaud's vast output comprises a large number of choral works, apart from the operas, the most important being the cantatas *Pour louer le Seigneur* (1928), *Pan et Syrinx* (1934), *Cantate de la paix* (1937) and *Cantate de la guerre* (1940) both on texts by Claudel; *Naissance de Venus* (1949), as well as a number of liturgical works on Hebrew and French and Hebrew and English words.

Another work which made choral history in its way was Honegger's *Le Roi David* (1921) whose impact on the French musical scene at the time was comparable to that of William Walton's *Belshazzar's Feast* in England some ten years later. Described as a 'dramatic oratorio', and scored for mixed chorus, woodwind, brass, double-bass, piano, harmonium and percussion, *King David* is laid out in twenty-seven episodes, vividly scored in an idiom which is largely polytonal, and is most effective in performance. Other important choral works by Honegger are *Judith*, *Jeanne d'Arc au bûcher*, *La danse des morts*, *Chant de la Libération* and *Une Cantate de Noël*.

Reflecting rather a different mood from that of any of the above works, Poulenc's choral compositions are mainly on religious texts, and the writing tends to be homophonic rather than contrapuntal and generally less aggressive. His three most important liturgical works are, as already mentioned, the Stabat Mater, Gloria and *Sept Répons des Ténèbres*; noteworthy, too, are the *Litanies à la Vierge Noire de Rocamadour*, the Mass, *Exultate Deo* and *Salve Regina*; all scored for unaccompanied chorus. Among the secular works are the two books of *Chansons françaises*, the cantata *Figure Humaine* (see Chapter 7), and the cantata for chorus and orchestra *Sécheresse* (text by Edward James).

Among other contemporary French composers who have enriched the current choral repertory in different ways are Messiaen (*Trois petites liturgies de la présence divine* and *Cinq Rechants*); Jean Françaix (*L'Apocalypse*); André Jolivet (*La tentation dernière de Jeanne d'Arc*); Henry Barraud (*Le Testament de Villon* and *Le Mystère des Saints Innocents*); Manuel Rosenthal (*Saint François d'Assise*).

From the foregoing summary review of some of the outstanding choral works in twentieth-century French music it will be seen that, even if at the present time this particular field tends to be neglected by contemporary composers of the avant-garde, choral music has nevertheless held a distinguished place in the repertory during the last half-century.

There are few, if any, great regional choirs, such as exist in England, but choral singing is encouraged in French *lycées*, and in most of the universities, and good work is done by the *Chorale des Jeunesses musicales*. A small, but highly proficient choral ensemble, specialising in contemporary music, and frequently representing France abroad, was founded and is directed today by Marcel Couraud; and in Paris the choirs attached to the two main broadcasting orchestras of the O.R.T.F., notably the Chœur Yvonne Gouverné, together with the Elizabeth Brasseur Chorale, are probably the finest in the country. Mention should also be made of the *Chanteurs de Saint-Gervais* (founded by Charles Bordes) and *La manécanterie des petits chanteurs à la Croix de Bois* for church and Gregorian music.

EPILOGUE

The picture I have tried to trace of music and musical life in France during the last half-century can only be, as I am only too well aware, in the nature of a sketch in which many details are inevitably lacking. One fact emerges, however, and that is that from 1900 to the beginning of the second world war, France, more than any other country, represented all that was best and most vital in twentieth-century music. It would indeed be no exaggeration to say that during this period French music and modern music had become synonymous; and the period saw a rare flowering of genius as well as of many great and varied talents. After two world wars the situation today is, not surprisingly, rather more confused, though there seems to be no reason to suppose that it is not fundamentally healthy. It would be, of course, unreasonable at this stage to hope for a repetition of the great renaissance in French music that reached its climax half-way through the century; and to expect another Fauré, another Debussy, another Ravel to appear during our generation or the next would, indeed, be to ask for more, perhaps, than we deserve. And perhaps for more than the evidence before us entitles us to expect.

For music everywhere is passing through a new and troubled phase—a phase of exploration in which the goal to be attained must often seem to the explorer as ill-defined as it is incomprehensible to the onlooker. In other words, the gulf between the creative artist and his public tends to grow wider every day. Composers are fumbling for a new language or, at least, a new vocabulary—and, only too conscious of the weight of tradition behind them, are torn between a dread of being considered reactionary and a desire to worship at the altar of unknown gods. They are right to be unwilling to follow like sheep in well-beaten paths; but there are signs today that in the keen competition to discover new idioms, new systems, new techniques, the means will be cultivated too often for their own sake, while the end which they should be serving, that is to say, the art of music itself, is sometimes in danger of being forgotten or ignored. Not only in France, but in other countries as well, the young composer in this uneasy, unsettled world in which we live is inclined to clutch desperately at some new formula, some new system, which has at least the merit of being untried. Then follows a period of trial-by-error, at the end of which he may emerge confident that he has found the Way—although, of course, it may be some time before he gets the cautious critics and the long-suffering public to agree with him.

This is, of course, the main cause of the misunderstanding, incomprehension and even hostility aroused by a great deal of contemporary music—the barrier that exists between the musician and his public. Obviously composers themselves are partly to blame for this—many extremists seem to be working in complete isolation today, and to have no desire even to establish communication with the rest of humanity. On the other hand, the public—what may be called the musically-minded public—can also be reproached for their lack of interest in contemporary music generally, their inertia, and unwillingness to go even half-way to meet, or at least to try to understand what contemporary composers are trying to do.

This, of course, is nothing new. Throughout the ages great creative artists have always been ahead of their time and have met with incomprehension, so true is it that, as Jean Cocteau once observed[1]: 'When a work of art appears to be in advance of its period, it is really the period that has lagged behind the work of art'. So there is no need to end this survey on a pessimistic note. The twentieth century so far has, as we have seen, been a wonderfully fertile epoch so far as French music is concerned; and, in spite of certain aberrations here and there, it is clear that there is plenty of healthy creative activity in France

[1] See: *Le Coq et l'Arlequin.*

today, and a questing spirit of exploration and serious endeavour which I venture to think augurs well for the future. So much vitality, so much enthusiasm, so much intelligence can surely not be wasted. French music, like France herself, has been through testing periods before now; but like the Phoenix, its powers of recuperation are legendary; and if ever there have been ashes, I think the flame is still there, and will continue to burn for many generations to come.

SELECTIVE BIBLIOGRAPHY

BERNARD, SUZANNE: *Mallarmé et la musique*, Paris, 1959

BOULEZ, PIERRE: *Relevés d'apprenti*, Paris, 1966 (Eng. Trans. New York, 1968)

CALVOCORESSI, M. D.: *Musicians' Gallery*, London, 1933

CHAILLEY, JACQUES: *40,000 ans de musique*, Paris, 1961 (Eng. Trans. London & New York, 1964)

COCTEAU, JEAN: *Le Coq et l'Arlequin*, Paris, 1918

COOPER, MARTIN: *French music*, London, 1951

CORTOT, ALFRED: *La musique française de piano*, Paris, 1948

DAVIES, LAURENCE: *The Gallic muse*, London, 1967; New York, 1968

DEANE, BASIL: *Albert Roussel*, London and New York, 1961

DÉCAUDIN, MICHEL: (Ed.) *Apollinaire et la musique*, Stavelot, 1967

DIETSCHY, MARCEL: *La passion de Claude Debussy*, Neuchâtel, 1962

DUKAS, PAUL: *Les écrits de Paul Dukas*

DUMESNIL, RENÉ: *La musique en France entre les deux guerres*, Paris, 1946

DURAND, JACQUES: *Lettres de Claude Debussy à son éditeur*, Paris, 1927

EMMANUEL, MAURICE: *Pelléas et Mélisande de Debussy*, Paris, 1950

GOLÉA, ANTOINE: *Esthétique de la musique contemporaine*, Paris, 1945; *20 ans de musique contemporaine*, Paris, 1962

HODEIR, ANDRÉ: *Since Debussy* (Trans.), London, 1961

LESURE, FRANÇOIS: (Ed.) *Claude Debussy: textes et documents inédits* (Société française de musicologie), Paris, 1962

LOCKSPEISER, EDWARD: *Debussy: his life and mind* (2 vols.), London and New York, 1962; (Ed.) *Claude Debussy: lettres inédites à André Caplet*, Monaco, 1962; (Ed.) *Debussy et Edgar Poe*, Monaco, 1960

LONG, MARGUERITE: *Au piano avec Claude Debussy*, Paris, 1960

MELLERS, WILFRID: *Caliban reborn*, London and New York, 1968

MEYLAN, PIERRE: *Les écrivains et la musique*, Lausanne, 1952

MILHAUD, DARIUS: *Notes sans musique*, Paris, 1949

MYERS, ROLLO: *Erik Satie*, London, 1948 (reprinting); Paris, 1959; N. York, 1968; *Debussy*, London, 1948 (o.p.); *Ravel: Life and works*, London & New York, 1960

OUELLETTE, FERNAND: *Edgard Varèse*, Paris, 1966 (Eng. Trans. New York, 1968)

PIROUÉ, GEORGES: *Proust et la musique du devenir*, Paris, 1962

ROUTH, FRANCIS: *Contemporary music*, London, 1968

ROY, JEAN: *Musique française: présences contemporaines*, Paris, 1962

SAMUEL, CLAUDE: *Entretiens avec Olivier Messiaen*, Paris, 1967

SCHAEFFER, PIERRE: *Traité des objets musicaux*, Paris, 1966; *A la recherche d'une musique concrète*, Paris, 1952

SHATTUCK, ROGER: *The Banquet Years*, London 1959.

SUARÈS, ANDRÉ: *Debussy*, Paris, 1936

SUCKLING, NORMAN: *Fauré*, London, 1946

VALÉRY, PAUL: *Pièces sur l'art*, Paris, 1934

WEBER, EDITH: (Ed.) *Debussy et l'évolution de la musique au XXe siècle* (Centre national de la recherche scientifique), Paris, 1965

WILENSKI, R. H.: *Modern French painters*, London, 1940; New York, 1968

GENERAL REFERENCE

Histoire de la musique (vol. II), *Encyclopédie de la Pléiade*, Paris, 1963.

INDEX

Important page references are given in bold figures.